Mozart's

THE MARRIAGE OF FIGARO
OPERA CLASSICS LIBRARY™

Edited by Burton D. Fisher
Principal lecturer, *Opera Journeys Lecture Series*

Opera Journeys™ Publishing / Coral Gables, Florida

OPERA CLASSICS LIBRARY ™

• Aida • The Barber of Seville • La Bohème • Carmen
• Cavalleria Rusticana • Così fan tutte • Don Giovanni
• Don Pasquale • The Elixir of Love • Elektra
• Eugene Onegin • Exploring Wagner's Ring • Falstaff
• Faust • The Flying Dutchman • Hansel and Gretel
• L'Italiana in Algeri • Julius Caesar • Lohengrin
• Lucia di Lammermoor • Macbeth • Madama Butterfly
• The Magic Flute • Manon • Manon Lescaut
• The Marriage of Figaro • A Masked Ball • The Mikado
• Otello • I Pagliacci • Porgy and Bess • The Rhinegold
• Rigoletto • Der Rosenkavalier • Salome • Samson and Delilah
• Siegfried • The Tales of Hoffmann • Tannhäuser
• Tosca • La Traviata • Il Trovatore • Turandot
• Twilight of the Gods • The Valkyrie

WEB SITE: www.operajourneys.com   E MAIL: operaj@bellsouth.net

"Opera to me comes before anything else..."

-Wolfgang Amadeus Mozart

Contents

a *Prelude*........
to OPERA CLASSICS LIBRARY's
THE MARRIAGE OF FIGARO

The Marriage of Figaro has proven to be one of the greatest masterpieces of comedy with music. Mozart's musical characterizations are ingenious; his melodies are enormously faithful to character and situation, contain charm, a perfection of form, and an utter spontaneity. Moreover, the music sparkles with all the wit and gaiety of Beaumarchais's humorous work, and certainly, much praise must be conceded to Lorenzo da Ponte's shrewdly contrived libretto.

OPERA CLASSICS LIBRARY explores the greatness and magic of Mozart's *The Marriage of Figaro*. The *Commentary and Analysis* offers pertinent biographical information about Mozart, his mind-set at the time of the opera's composition, the genesis of the opera, its premiere and performance history, and insightful story and character analysis.

The text also contains a *Brief Story Synopsis, Principal Characters in The Marriage of Figaro,* and a *Story Narrative with Music Highlight Examples,* the latter containing original music transcriptions that are interspersed appropriately within the story's dramatic exposition. In addition, the text includes a *Discography, Videography,* and a *Dictionary of Opera and Musical Terms.*

The *Libretto* for *The Marriage of Figaro* has been newly translated by the Opera Journeys staff with specific emphasis on retaining a literal translation, but also with the objective to provide a faithful translation in modern and contemporary English; in this way, the substance of the drama becomes more intelligible. To enhance educational and study objectives, the *Libretto* also contains music highlight examples interspersed within the drama.

The opera art form is the sum of many artistic expressions: theatrical drama, music, scenery, poetry, dance, acting and gesture. In opera, it is the composer who is the dramatist, using the emotive power of his music to express intense, human conflicts. Words evoke thought, but music provokes feelings; opera's sublime fusion of words, music and all the theatrical arts provides powerful theater, an impact on one's sensibilities that can reach into the very depths of the human soul. Mozart's *The Marriage of Figaro,* certainly a crown jewel of his glorious operatic and musical inventions, remains a masterpiece of the lyric theater, a tribute to the art form as well as to its ingenious composer.

Burton D. Fisher
Editor
OPERA CLASSICS LIBRARY

THE MARRIAGE OF FIGARO

"Le Nozze di Figaro"

Italian opera in four acts
by
Wolfgang Amadeus Mozart

Libretto by Lorenzo da Ponte after Beaumarchais's play
La Folle Journée ou Le Mariage de Figaro,
("The Crazy Day, or The Marriage of Figaro") 1784

Premiere:
Burgtheater, Vienna
May 1786

Commentary and Analysis

Wolfgang Amadeus Mozart — 1756 to 1791 — was born in Salzburg, Austria. His life-span was brief, but his musical achievements were phenomenal and monumental. Mozart has become one of the most important and inspired composers in Western history: music seemed to gush forth from his creative soul like fresh water from a spring. With his early death at the age of thirty-five, one can only dream of the musical treasures that might have materialized from his music pen.

Along with such masters as Johann Sebastian Bach and Ludwig van Beethoven, Mozart was one of those three "immortals" of classical music. Superlatives about Mozart are inexhaustible: Tchaikovsky called him "the music Christ"; Haydn, a contemporary who revered and idolized him, claimed he was the best composer he ever knew; Schubert wept over "the impressions of a brighter and better life he had imprinted on our souls"; Schumann wrote that there were some things in the world about which nothing could be said: much of Shakespeare, pages of Beethoven, and Mozart's last symphony, the forty-first.

Richard Wagner, who exalted the emotive power of the orchestra in his music dramas, assessed Mozart's symphonies: "He seemed to breathe into his instruments the passionate tones of the human voice ... and thus raised the capacity of orchestral music for expressing the emotions to a height where it could represent the whole unsatisfied yearning of the heart."

Although Mozart's career was short, his musical output was phenomenal by any standard: more than 600 works that include forty-one symphonies, twenty-seven piano concertos, more than thirty string quartets, many acclaimed quintets, world-famous violin and flute concertos, momentous piano and violin sonatas, and, of course, a substantial legacy of sensational operas.

Mozart's father, Leopold, an eminent musician and composer in his own right, became the teacher and inspiration to his exceptionally talented and incredibly gifted prodigy child. The young Mozart quickly demonstrated a thorough command of the technical resources of musical composition: at age three he went to the harpsichord and played tunes he had just heard; at age four he began composing his own music; at age six he gave his first public concert; by age twelve he had written ten symphonies, a cantata, and an opera; and at age thirteen he toured Italy, where in Rome, he astonished the music world by writing out the full score of a complex religious composition after one hearing.

Mozart's musical style and the music of the late eighteenth century Classical era are virtually synonymous. The goal of Classical era music was to conform to specific standards and forms, to be succinct, clear, and well balanced, but at the same time, to develop musical ideas to an emotionally satisfying fullness. As a quintessential Classicist, Mozart's music has become universally extolled; his music represents an outpouring of memorable graceful melody that is combined with formal, contrapuntal ingenuity.

During the late eighteenth-century, a musician's livelihood depended solidly on patronage from royalty and the aristocracy. Mozart and his sister, Nannerl, a skilled harpsichord player, frequently toured Europe together and performed at the courts of Austria, England, France, and Holland. But in Mozart's native Salzburg, Austria, he felt artistically oppressed by the Archbishop and decided to relocate to Vienna. There, he received first-rate appointments and financial security that emanated from the adoring support of both the Empress Maria Thèrése, and later her son, the Emperor Joseph II. Opera legend relates the story of a post-performance meeting between Emperor Joseph II and Mozart in which the Emperor commented: "Too beautiful for our ears and too many notes, my dear Mozart." Mozart replied: "Exactly as many as necessary, Your Majesty."

As the young Mozart began to compose his first operas in the mid-eighteenth century, the German composer Christoph Wilibald Gluck (1714-1787), the art form's second great reformer after Metastasio, had established new rules for modern music drama. Gluck returned to the ideals of opera's founders — the Camerata — and believed that musico-dramatic integrity and the truthful expression of human emotions and passions were synonymous.

Gluck rebelled against the excesses which had seized the existing *opera seria* traditions: intricate plots, flowery speeches, and grandiose climaxes had become excessively ornate and superfluous, causing the truthful expression of the human experience to become increasingly remote. As such, Gluck departed from the mannerisms and pompous artificiality of the Italian traditions which had dominated the art form, and banished the excesses and abuses of singers, in particular, their florid *da capo* arias.

Gluck was seeking a dramatic truth in operatic expression which he would achieve through greater simplicity, clarity and naturalism. In his search for that musico-dramatic ideal, he brought to his music a touching sentiment and a wealth of expressive, emotional feeling: "Restrict music to its true office by means of expression and by following situations of the story."

With Gluck, the unending debate was revitalized between supporters of the primacy of the opera libretto, and the supporters of the primacy of the music. But in Gluck's perception, music and text had to be integrated into a coherent whole. With Gluck's reforms, the lyric theater progressed into another stage of evolution as it advanced toward musico-dramatic maturity.

Gluck's 46 operas, in particular, his *Orfeo ed Euridice* (1762), and *Alceste* (1767), became the models for the next generation of opera composers: all of his operas were distinguished by a pronounced dramatic intensity, enriched musical inventions, a poetic expressiveness, and an intimate integration between their music and text. Mozart, following Gluck's guidelines, became the rejuvenator of the opera art form during the latter half of the eighteenth century.

Mozart said: "Opera to me comes before everything else." He composed his operas in all of the existing genres and traditions: the Italian *opera seria* and *opera buffa*, and the German *singspiel*.

During Mozart's time, the Italians set the international standards for opera: Italian was the universal language of music and opera, and Italian opera was what Mozart's Austrian audiences and most of the rest of Europe wanted most. Therefore, even though Mozart was an Austrian, his country part of the German Holy Roman Empire, most of his operas were written in Italian.

Opera seria defines the style of serious Italian operas whose subjects and themes dealt primarily with mythology, history, and Greek tragedy. In this genre, the music drama usually portrayed an heroic or tragic conflict that typically involved a moral dilemma, such as love vs. duty, and usually resolved happily with due reward for rectitude, loyalty, and unselfishness.

Before Mozart, *opera serias* (baroque) were grandiose and elaborate productions, their cardboard-style characters rigid and pretentious, and their scores saturated with florid *da capo* arias, few ensembles, and almost no chorus. But Mozart would follow Gluck's guidelines and strive for more profound dramatic integrity. He parted from existing traditions and endowed his own works with a greater fusion between recitative and aria, the use of accompanied recitatives, many ensembles, and greater use of the orchestra.

Mozart's most renowned *opera serias* are *Idomeneo* (1781), and his last opera, *La Clemenza di Tito* ("The Clemency of Titus"), the latter a work commissioned to celebrate the coronation in Prague of the Emperor Leopold II as King of Bohemia.

Opera buffa had its roots in popular entertainment: its predecessors were the Italian *commedia dell'arte* and the *intermezzi*. The *commedia dell'arte* theatrical conventions evolved during the Renaissance when strolling players presented satire, irony, and parody about real-life situations. They ridiculed every aspect of their society and its institutions; they characterized humorous or hypocritical situations involving cunning servants, scheming doctors, and duped masters. Similarly, *intermezzi,* or interludes performed between the acts of dramatic plays, provided that same comedy, satire and parody.

Most of the characters in Beaumarchais's original "Figaro trilogy," the literary basis for Rossini's *The Barber of Seville* and Mozart's *The Marriage of Figaro*, have antecedents in the *commedia dell'arte*. Figaro himself was loosely based on the then popular *commedia dell'arte* character of Harlequin, an athletic, graceful, cunning valet and ladies' man who claimed noble birth. Likewise, the Dr. Bartolo character was inspired by the character of Pantelone, a man who prided his expertise on many subjects, but one who actually knew very little and was always entrapped by his own arrogance and vanity. The Marcellina character in *The Marriage of Figaro* is perhaps the only character not based on *commedia dell'arte:* she is one of those old rapacious spinsters plucked out of classical Roman comedies.

Opera buffa, nurtured by the *commedia dell'arte* and *intermezzi* genres, became a very popular Italian opera genre. Its first popular incarnation was in Giovanni Pergolesi's *La Serva Padrona* (1733), a work with only three characters, but a quintessential model of the genre: it contained lively and catchy tunes which underscored the antics of a servant tricking an old bachelor into marriage.

The greatness of all art forms is that they express the soul and zeitgeist of their times. The eighteenth century was dominated by the Enlightenment, a philosophic movement marked by a profound rejection of traditional social, religious, and political ideas, and an emphasis on rationalism; the Enlightenment inspired a rebirth in the ideals of human dignity and freedom.

Opera buffa provided a convenient theatrical vehicle in which those Enlightenment ideals of democracy and humanism could be expressed in art: *opera buffa* became an operatic incarnation of political populism. The ruling aristocracies identified and even became flattered by the exalted personalities, gods, and heroes portrayed in the pretentious pomp and formality of the *opera seria.* In contrast, *opera buffa's* satire and humor provided an arena to portray very human characters in everyday situations. But more importantly, the genre presented an opportunity to examine and express class distinctions and the frustrations of society's lower classes.

As such, *opera buffa* became synonymous with the spirit of the Enlightenment and the Classical era of music: the genre was enthusiastically championed by such renowned progressive thinkers as Rousseau; its music was intrinsically more natural, and its melodies elegant, yet emotionally restrained.

Mozart delighted in portraying themes dealing with the inspired ideals of the Enlightenment. He was living and composing during a monumental historical period of social upheaval and ideological transition. It was a time in which the common man fought for his rights against the tyranny and oppression of the aristocracies. In particular, *The Marriage of Figaro* contains all of the era's social and political conflicts and tensions: its primary theme is its portrayal of servants who are more clever than their selfish, unscrupulous, and arrogant masters. Because of the comic effectiveness of its underlying political and social themes, *The Marriage of Figaro* has earned the accolade of the perfect *opera buffa.* Napoleon would later conclude that *Marriage,* both the Mozart opera and Beaumarchais's original play, represented the "Revolution in action."

Mozart's *opera buffas* range from his youthful works, *La Finta Semplici* (1768) and *La Finta Giardineria* (1775), to his monumental *buffa* classics composed with the renowned librettist, Lorenzo Da Ponte. The Mozart-Da Ponte collaboration produced *The Marriage of Figaro,* ("Le Nozze di Figaro") (1786)), described by both composer and librettist as a *commedia per musica* ("comedy with music"); *Don Giovanni,* (1787), technically an *opera buffa* but designated a *dramma giocoso,* ("humorous drama" or "playful play"), that is essentially a combination of both the *opera buffa* and *opera seria* genres; and *Così fan tutte,* ("Thus do all women behave") (1789), another blend of genres for which nothing could be more laudatory than the renowned musicologist William Mann's conclusion that *Così fan tutte* contains "the most captivating music ever composed."

Nevertheless, although Mozart was writing in the Italian *opera buffa* genre and in the Italian language, Italians have historically shunned his Italian works, claiming that they were not "Italian" enough; contemporary productions of Mozart "Italian" operas in Italy are rare events.

Mozart also composed operas in the German *singspiel* genre, a style very similar to Italian *opera buffa* that generally defines comic opera containing spoken dialogue instead of accompanied recitative. Mozart's most popular German *singspiel* operas are: *Die Zauberflöte* ("The Magic Flute") and *Die Entführung aus dem Serail* ("The Abduction from the Seraglio.")

Mozart wrote over 18 operas, among them: *Bastien and Bastienne* (1768); *La Finta Semplice* (1768); *Mitridate, Rè di Ponto* (1770); *Ascanio in Alba* (1771); *Il Sogno di Scipione* (1772); *Lucio Silla* (1772); *La Finta Giardiniera* (1774); *Idomeneo, Rè di Creta* (1781); *Die Entführung aus dem Serail* ("The Abduction from the Seraglio") (1782); *Der Schauspieldirektor* (1786); *Le Nozze di Figaro,* ("The Marriage of Figaro") (1786); *Don Giovanni* (1787); *Così fan tutte* (1790); *Die Zauberflöte* ("The Magic Flute") (1791); *La Clemenza di Tito* (1791).

M ozart was unequivocal about his opera objectives: "In an opera, poetry must be the obedient daughter of the music." But although Mozart gave priority to his music, he indeed took great care in selecting his text and poetry, hammering relentlessly at his librettists to be sure they produced words that could be illuminated and transcended by his music. To an opera composer of such incredible genius as Mozart, words performed through his music could express what language alone had exhausted.

Opera portrays the emotions and behavior of human beings, and its success lies in its ability to convey and intensify human character through the emotive power of its music.

Mozart understood humanity and ingeniously translated his incredible human insight through his musical language. Mozart became one of the greatest masters of musical characterization and musical portraiture. Like Shakespeare, he ingeniously translated "dramatic truth" through his music; his musical characterizations portray complex human emotions, passions, and feelings, and bare the souls of his characters with truthful representations of universal humanity; in those characterizations, the composer exposes the entire spectrum of human virtues, aspirations, inconsistencies, peculiarities, flaws, and foibles. Although Mozart reveals the souls of his characters, he rarely suggests any puritanical judgment or moralization of their behavior and actions.That focus on action rather than philosophy prompted Beethoven to lament that in *Don Giovanni* and *The Marriage of Figaro,* Mozart had squandered his genius on immoral and licentious subjects.

Nevertheless, it is that spotlight on the individual that makes Mozart's characterizations a bridge between eighteenth and nineteenth century operas. Before Mozart, in the *opera seria* genre, operas portrayed abstract emotion; often, the dramatic form imitated the style of the ancient Greek theater in which an individual's passions and the dramatic situations would generally transfer to the chorus for either narration, commentary, or summation. But Mozart was anticipating the transition to the Romantic movement that was to begin soon after his death. He discarded the masks hiding the inner human soul; his music endows his characters with profound human sentiments and feelings, and distinctive and recognizable musical personalities.

Thus, Mozart clearly perceived the vast possibilities of the operatic form as a means of musically creating characterization: in his operas, great and small persons move, think, and breathe on a very truthful human level, and there are extraordinary and insightful portrayals of the conduct and character of real and complex humanity. It is in the interaction between those characters themselves, particularly in ensembles that are almost symphonic in grandeur, that an individual character's emotions, passions, feelings, and reactions stand out in high relief.

As a consequence, for over two-hundred years, Mozart's treasured characterizations have captivated opera audiences: *Don Giovanni's* Donna Anna, Donna Elvira, Zerlina, Masetto, Leporello, and Don Giovanni himself; *The Marriage of Figaro's* Count and Countess, Cherubino, Susanna, and Figaro. All of these Mozartian characters are profoundly human: they act with passion as well as sentiment, yet they always retain that special Mozartian dignity.

In the end, like Shakespeare, Mozart's characterizations have become timeless representations of humanity; they can be great, or they can be flawed. Nevertheless, Mozart's characterizations are as contemporary in the 20th-century as they were in the later part of the 18th century, even though costumes and customs may have changed. So *The Marriage of Figaro's* predatory Count Almaviva, attempting to exercise his feudal right of *droit de seigneur,* may hypothetically be no different than his 20th century counterpart: a successful, if not arrogant executive, legally forbidden, yet desiring to bed his illegal alien housekeeper against her wishes.

In order to portray, communicate, and truthfully mirror the human condition, Mozart became a magician in developing and inventing various techniques within his unique musical language. He expresses those human qualities not only through distinguishing melody, but also through the specific essence of certain key signatures, as well as rhythm, tempo, pitch, accent and speech inflection.

As an example, each musical key has an inherent power to convey a particular mood and effect. Mozart often used G major as the key to convey rustic life and the common people: A major as the seductive key for sensuous love scenes. In *Don Giovanni*, D minor, Mozart's key for *Sturm und Drang* (storm and stress), appears solemnly in the Overture and in its colossal final scene. When characters are in trouble, their key is far removed from the home key: as they get out of trouble, they return to the home key, reducing the tension.

In both Mozart's *Don Giovanni* and *The Marriage of Figaro*, social classes clash, but with sentiment and insight. Mozart's characterizations range from underdogs to demigods, but in particular, when he deals with peasants and the lower classes, his music is subtle, compassionate, and loving. Therefore, Mozart's heroes are those bright characters who occupy the lower social levels, those Figaros, Susannas, and Zerlinas, characters whom he ennobles with poignant musical portrayals of their complex personal emotions, feelings, hopes, sadness, envy, passion, revenge, and yearning for love.

Mozart's theatrical genius was his ability to express truly human qualities in music. His character inventions possess a universal and sublime uniqueness: in the end, Mozart achieved an incomparable immortality for himself as well as his character creations.

The commission for *The Marriage of Figaro* was received from Mozart's faithful patron, Emperor Joseph II of Austria. In 1786, its premiere year, the opera experienced triumphant productions in both Vienna and Prague, even though, quite naturally, the aristocracy deemed its libretto as having emanated from the depths of vulgarity. Nevertheless, with respect to its Prague premiere, the city was not directly under the control of the imperial Hapsburgs, and, therefore, any censorship or restriction of its underlying thematic elements was limited, if nonexistent.

Mozart had chosen Lorenzo da Ponte as his librettist: that peripatetic scholar, entrepreneur, and erstwhile crony of the notorious Casanova de Seingalt, reputedly a contributor of sections of the later *Don Giovanni* libretto.

Lorenzo da Ponte, nee Emmanuel Conegliano, was born in Italy in 1749, and died in America in 1838. He converted from Judaism, and after his baptism took the name da Ponte to honor the Bishop of Ceneda. Da Ponte aspired to a life in the Church, but seminary life failed. Afterwards, he embarked on a picaresque life that bears an uncanny resemblance to that of his libertine romantic hero, Don Giovanni.

Da Ponte was always involved in scandals and intrigues. At one time he was banished from Venice; at another, he was forced to leave England under threat of imprisonment for his financial difficulties. Finally, in 1805, he emigrated to the United States and taught Italian at Columbia University, where he introduced Italian literary classics to America. He later became an opera impresario, who in 1825, may have been the first to present Italian opera in the United States.

In Da Ponte's haughty biography, *Extract from the Life of Lorenzo Da Ponte* (1819), he explains why Mozart chose him as his inspirational poet: "Because Mozart knew very well that the success of an opera depends, first of all, on the poet than a composer, who is, in regard to drama, what a painter is in regard to colors, and can never do without effect, unless excited and animated by the words of a poet, whose province is to choose a subject susceptible of variety, movement, and action, to prepare, to suspend, to bring about the catastrophe, to exhibit characters interesting, comic, well supported, and calculated for stage effect, to write his *recitativo* short, but substantial, his airs various, new, and well situated; and his fine verses easy, harmonious, and almost singing of themselves….."

Certainly, in Da Ponte's librettos for three of Mozart's operas, he indeed ascribed religiously to those literary and dramatic disciplines and qualities he so eloquently described and congratulated himself for in his autobiography.

The Da Ponte-Mozart source for *The Marriage of Figaro* was the trilogy of plays written by Pierre Augustin Caron de Beaumarchais (1732-1799). Beaumarchais was as colorful a real-life character as those he created in his plays.

He was the son of a clockmaker and initially followed in his father's footsteps; he was subsequently appointed clockmaker and watchmaker to the court of Louis XV. He was also a musician; he was a self-taught student of guitar, flute, and harp, composed works for these instruments, and eventually became the harp teacher to the King's daughters. After marrying the widow of a court official in 1756, he was elevated to the status of a nobleman, took the name Beaumarchais, and bought the office of secretary to the king.

In 1763, France was still seeking revenge for its loss of Canada, and was observing with great interest the development of the American "resistance movement." In support, the French government offered covert aid to the American rebels, but they were determined to keep France out of the war until an opportune moment. Nevertheless, in the pivotal year 1776, a fictitious company was set up under the direction of the author Pierre Augustin Caron de Beaumarchais, its purpose, to funnel military supplies and sell arms to the rebellious American colonists.

Beaumarchais's specific fame and legacy are his literary achievements: the comedic theatrical trilogy, which includes *Le Barbier de Séville, ou La précaution inutile* (1775), ("The Barber of Seville, or the Useless Precaution"), *Le mariage de Figaro, ou La folle journée* (1784), ("The Marriage of Figaro, or the Crazy Day"), and the final installment, *L'autre Tartuffe, ou La Mère Coupable,* ("The Guilty Mother") (1792).

In these plays, Beaumarchais weaves together a cast of thinly disguised heroes, lower class characters whose only means to survive is though imagination and ingenuity. None is more admirable than Figaro — Beaumarchais himself — who is a master of sabotage and intrigue, and a clever and enterprising "man for all seasons." Figaro is opposed by villains and tormentors who are simultaneously in continuous conflict with one another: Figaro's antagonists are all members of the upper classes.

Figaro's witty and high-handed attitude toward his aristocratic master, Count Almaviva, in those days, a virtual omen of revolution, is clearly defined in Beaumarchais's play when Figaro speaks about the Count: "What have you done to earn so many honors? You have taken the trouble to be born, that's all."

Beaumarchais's plays reflected the winds of change stirred by the Enlightenment: they satirized the French ruling class and reflected the growing lower class dissatisfaction with the nobility in the years preceding the French Revolution. Both Beaumarchais's *Le Barbier de Séville* and *Le marriage de Figaro,* in their caustic satire of prevailing social and political conditions, flatter the lower classes, and castigate the upper class nobility.

Beaumarchais's heroic output, the "Figaro trilogy," or the "Almaviva trilogy," indeed represent an historical canvas of the late eighteenth century zeitgeist. The plays sum up the era and overflow with social and political conflicts and tensions. In essence, they became the essential personification of the forthcoming French Revolution, which they not only reflect, but even influenced, inspired, and consciously or unconsciously set into motion. In these plays, the *ancien regime* is seen in declining grandeur and impending doom; social change and transition are imminent.

All of the plays center around the colorful character of the factotum Figaro, a jack-of-all-trades, whose savvy and ingenuity serve as the symbol of class revolt against the aristocracy. *Le barbier de Séville,* originally written by Beaumarchais as an opera libretto for the Opéra-Comique, was banned for two years before it was finally performed in 1775; it was a failure at its first performance, but it was catapulted to success after later revisions. King Louis XVI briefly imprisoned Beaumarchais for his blasphemous writings, but later acceded to public pressure and placated him. In an ironic twist, the King agreed to a gala performance of *Le barber de Seville* at Versailles: his wife, Marie-Antoinette portrayed Rosine, and the future Charles X, portrayed Figaro. The second part of the trilogy, *Le marriage de Figaro* became such a triumph that it ran for eighty-six consecutive performances. Again, Louis XVI attempted to prohibit performances of *Le marriage*, but the masses, not in a mood to be trifled with in those times, demanded and received performances.

Mozart's opera *The Marriage of Figaro,* and later, Rossini's opera *Il Barbiere di Siviglia,* ("The Barber of Seville") (1816), would eventually assure literary immortality for Beaumarchais's masterpieces. It is noteworthy that each one of Beaumarchais's plays ends in a marriage, but not everyone lives happily ever after: each play seems to resolve more darker than the one before. In Beaumarchais's final installment, *L'autre Tartuffe, ou la La Mère Coupable,* ("The Guilty Mother") (1792), the Countess Almaviva has a child by Cherubino. Mozart died before its premiere, and one is tempted to speculate how Mozart would have darkened that episode with his music had he attacked an opera on the subject.

Mozart's *The Marriage of Figaro* antedates Rossini's *Il Barbiere di Siviglia* by thirty years. Rossini's work essentially owes its provenance to another opera based on Beaumarchais: Paisello's *Barbiere di Siviglia* (1780). But it was Rossini's admiration for Mozart's *Marriage* that strongly persuaded him to create his *Barber* opera, a work now acclaimed as the greatest *opera buffa* ever written, as well as the perfect companion piece to Mozart's *Marriage.*

Nevertheless, in Rossini's *Barber,* the political and social undercurrents of the late eighteenth century are understated. By 1816, the premiere year of *Barber*, the French Revolution had already become indelibly inscribed in history, and the Congress of Vienna had just implemented a new status quo for Europe. In fact, Rossini's libretto was considered so inoffensive to the aristocracy that his librettist, Cesare Sterbini, easily recieved the approval of the Roman censor. Although censorship remained a powerful instrument for suppression, the government made no effort or pretext to suppress it.

As it turned out, opposition to Rossini's opera was purely personal, cloaked behind the opera public's devotion to the venerated Paisello, the composer of the first *Barber* opera; Paisello was still alive and revered by the public.

In truth, these two Figaro operas are perfect companions. Although the later Rossini work has none of the deep and tender sentiment which underlies so much of Mozart's creation, from a comic viewpoint, Rossini's work inherently deals with a more humorous phase of the entire trilogy: it possesses intrinsic humor, frolic, and vivacity as it portrays the Count Almaviva's adventures with Figaro as they outwit Dr. Bartolo and carry off the mischievous Rosina.

But in contrast, *The Marriage of Figaro* story offers a depiction of the transformation of the Count after his marriage to Rosina: his intrigues, suspicions, and philanderings. The differences are certainly evident in Rossini's *Barber,* where the youthful and impetuous characters have an elemental freshness, but in Mozart, they have matured, become domesticated, and certainly have transcended youthful innocence. Nevertheless, these two operas are "marriages made in operatic heaven."

In addition to Mozart and Rossini, Beaumarchais's comedies were made into operas by Friedrich Ludwig Benda in *Der Barbier von Sevilla*; Paerrs in *Il nuovo Figaro*; and of course, in Paisello's *The Barber of Seville.*

B eaumarchais's heroic "Figaro trilogy" deals with despicable aspects of human character; transformation of the existing 18th century social structure was the very foundations of Enlightenment idealism, and that yearning for change became the undercurrent that led to the French Revolution.

The engines that drive the plots of *The Marriage of Figaro* — and *Don Giovanni* — are the moral foibles and peccadillos of aristocratic men: Count Almaviva and Don Giovanni are the nobility, men who can almost be perceived by modern standards as criminals; men who are unstable, wildly libidinous, and men who feel themselves above moral law. Both operas focus on seduction; seduction that ends in hapless failure.

The class conflicts and their social and political realities, all unite and blend into a highly sophisticated battle of the sexes. *The Marriage* story takes place three years after the *Barber* story, and Count Almaviva has now become a predatory philanderer. Rosina, now the Countess, displays mature wisdom well beyond her youthful years. One part of the story revolves around Figaro's imminent marriage to Susanna. But the other part portrays the Count as a lecher, obsessed to seduce Susanna, even though he has abandoned his feudal right of *droit de signeur.*

Figaro and Susanna must use their ingenuity to thwart the Count's lascivious intentions. The lower classes become the heroes of the story, using their wiles, wit, determination, decency and love — and a little bit of luck — to tip the scales against upper class arrogance and power. In the process, these lower class characters become divinely articulate harbingers of revolution. Although da Ponte removed elements of Beaumarchais's original text that he considered potentially offensive, the irony is that Mozart unhesitatingly represents those very same ideas in his musical language with clarity and boldness.

Nevertheless, class relations are presented de facto, and the underlying implication is that status in the social hierarchy is an accident of fortune rather than a reflection of native worth: these themes are clearly woven into the musical fabric of *The Marriage of Figaro.*

The two main female characters in *The Marriage of Figaro,* Susanna and the Countess, are portrayed with brilliant musical contrast. In Mozart's later *Don Giovanni,* he would likewise provide a profound musical portrayal of diverse femininity in the contrasting characterizations of Donna Anna, Donna Elvira, and Zerlina.

Susanna is indeed the heroine of the story: she is multidimensional and complex, and possesses a profound instinctive intelligence. Like her Columbina forebears from the *commedia dell'arte,* and even Rosina from Beaumarchais's *Barbier.* She is a spirited character; she is sharp-witted, spunky, wily, and the master of irony. It is a brilliant climactic moment in the opera when she emerges from the closet and presents herself to the sword-wielding Count with feigned disingenuousness and masterful irony. But she also radiates assuredness and omniscience, whether in her conversations with the Countess, or in her attempts to fight off becoming a victim of the lecherous Count.

Susanna proves to be the one character in the opera who is stable and capable of sorting out everybody's troubles as well as her own. From the very beginning, she demonstrates her intuitive intelligence and insight when she opens Figaro's eyes to the Count's ulterior motives in placing their room so close to his quarters. But it is in the last act, when Mozart provides Susanna with that sensuous aria, "Deh viene non tardar," that she overwhelms Figaro with great tenderness and emotion. Susanna's aria is one of those magnificent moments in opera when action and time stand still, and sublime music intervenes to convey humanity's aspirations of love and happiness.

That other great female character in *The Marriage* is the Countess, a seemingly pathetic, wounded woman. She is prone to melancholy, but always exudes a profound spiritual, noble, and moral presence. Her dignity has been pitifully injured by the Count, but she never at anytime considers staining his honor by vengefully taking a lover. Subconsciously she understands her husband, but consciously she cannot accept the philandering of a man seemingly bored by his wife, and unaware that he is victimized by a massive mid-life crisis.

Mozart gave the Countess's two great arias in which she movingly expresses resignation but profound dignity: "Dov'e sono" and "Porgi amor:" Da Ponte's text for these arias are heartfelt expressions of a truly noble and aristocratic woman, but it is the emotive power of Mozart's music that reflects her true feelings and conveys genuine pathos.

The finale of Act II is perhaps one of Mozart's most monumental musical inventions and designs. It is an episode of some 150 pages of score that is perhaps without parallel in opera; its 20 minute length virtually makes it a play itself. In this finale, Mozart continuously uses a variety of key changes that serve to alter the mood and provide surprise upon surprise. Eventually, eight characters appear on stage, and the ensemble builds steadily, but never with a false climax, inconsistency, or artificial stroke.

The engine that drives the Act II finale is complex misunderstandings. Who is in the Countess's closet? (Is it Cherubino as both the Count and Countess presume?) What are the contents of the dropped paper? (Figaro has to be primed by Susanna through the Countess to learn that it is Cherubino's commission.) Is the Countess having a clandestine rendezvous with a lover? (The Count's obsession to know who wrote the anonymous note.) And, who jumped from the window into the garden?

The ensemble is inaugurated when the Count begins to break down the closet door, convinced that it is Cherubino who is hiding, and that he is the Countess's lover. The only two characters on stage, the Count and the Countess, begin an acrimonious exchange. The Count erupts in rage and becomes overbearing and intolerably aggressive. The Countess becomes flustered in her attempts to reason with him as she tries to persuade him of her innocence, but she compounds his outrage by admitting that Cherubino is indeed in the closet — and only half dressed.

The first surprise — to both the Count and Countess — is the emergence from the closet of Susanna, not Cherubino. Out of necessity, and recognizing a misunderstanding, the Count calms down, and has no other alternative than to ask his wife's forgiveness.

With Figaro's arrival, the ensemble builds to four characters. The Count, suspicious and confused, decides to question his wily valet, instinctively condemning him for being involved in the anonymous letter he received. And then the group becomes a quintet when the gardener Antonio arrives to announce that someone jumped out the window and ruined his flower bed.

The comic confusion augments and reaches a climax with the entrance of Don Basilio, Dr. Bartolo, and Marcellina, the latter arriving to claim that Figaro must marry her because he has not paid his debt to her.

In this ensemble, all the characters sing individually and also in ensemble. Through Mozart's genius, the ensemble fuses like a symphony, the music's incremental changes creating new dramatic moments that convey sensibilities, truths, and underlying subtleties. Mozart emphatically highlights each surprise and revelation with a change in key, rhythm, and tempo. As such, one feels and senses shock, nevertheless, the sequence maintains a sense of delicacy and playfulness, and always hints of new revelations.

In this finale of Act II, Mozart proved that he was ingeniously innovative. No one before him had attempted such a long, uninterrupted operatic ensemble. In the eighteenth century opera composers traditionally wrote short numbers, all strung together with recitatives or spoken dialogues. But in this ensemble that concludes Act II, its musical numbers are all welded and integrated as one unit.

The engine that drives the _Marriage_ story concerns an entire series of crises which evolve as a result of misunderstandings, a host of erroneous presumptions made from vaguely seen events, or overheard conversations not clearly understood. The characters are continually acting and reacting to their senses: they see and hear things from which they make presumptions, but they are never sure, and as a result, crises develop and envelop the characters.

Cherubino overheard the Count pressuring Susanna amorously; the Count overheard Basilio spread scandalous rumors about the Countess; the Count overheard Susanna proclaiming victory in Marcellina's suit against Figaro; Figaro believed he caught Susanna with the Count; and the Count believed he caught Figaro with the Countess. Conversations and misunderstandings drive the plot to its conclusion

Until the opera's conclusion, the conclusion to what Beaumarchais titled a "Crazy Day," each character suffers because of misjudgments. He assumes a truth but it is not a truth, only the result of a vague visual or aural perception.

The opera's finale is 15 minutes long and is devoted to the weaving and unweaving of the story's comical complications and mistaken identities. Beaumarchais was a master technician in injecting these plot complications into his play. But it was Mozart who provided the emotive power of the musical language to invent incredibly descriptive music to comment on the characters' inner feelings and sensibilities during these crises.

In *The Marriage of Figaro,* eyes and ears become the instruments of illusion and delusion. But illusion and delusion oppose reality and truth, the ultimate source of knowledge. At the conclusion of this masterpiece, knowledge is achieved, the imagined world becomes the real world, and unfounded perceptions and misunderstandings become reality and truth.

*T*he Marriage of Figaro is a social chronicle of its times. Its search for universal truth was originally penned by Beaumarchais, and later transformed into an opera libretto by Da Ponte. Ultimately, the story was endowed with incredible musical inventions by Mozart. It was the twilight of the Enlightenment, a time when humanity's craving for freedom and social justice would materialize and become engraved into Western history through events such as the storming of the Bastille and the French Revolution itself.

Mozart's music for *The Marriage of Figaro,* like its literary foundations, thunders for social reform, equality, and remains a lasting testament to humanity's greatest aspirations: freedom and justice.

Principal Characters in the Opera

Count Almaviva	Baritone
Countess Almaviva	Soprano
Figaro, the Count's valet	Baritone
Susanna, a maid to the Countess, betrothed to Figaro	Soprano
Cherubino, a young page	Soprano
Dr. Bartolo, a lawyer and physician	Bass
Marcellina, Dr. Bartolo's housekeeper	Contralto
Don Basilio, music master	Bass
Antonio, a gardener, and Susanna's uncle	Bass
Don Curzio, a lawyer	Tenor
Barbarina, Antonio's daughter	Soprano

TIME and PLACE: The 18th century.

The Count Almaviva's chateau in the
countryside near Seville

Brief Story Synopsis

In the first episode of the trilogy, *The Barber of Seville* story, the young Count Almaviva courts Rosina, luring her from the jealous and self-serving guardianship of Dr. Bartolo through a series of subterfuges, intrigues, and adventures, all engineered with the help of Figaro, Seville's illustrious barber, factotum, and jack-of-all-trades.

In the second episode, *The Marriage of Figaro,* Count Almaviva has married Rosina: she is now the Countess Almaviva; Figaro is the Count's valet, a reward he received for his services to the Count; and Dr. Bartolo has become the "doctor of the house." Dr. Bartolo seethes with revenge against Figaro for having outwitted him and enabling the Count to marry Rosina. Together with the housekeeper, Marcellina, who also harbors resentment toward Figaro, they conspire for vengeance against Figaro.

The noble Count Almaviva of *The Barber of Seville* story, has become transformed into a philanderer with amorous designs on Figaro's bride-to-be, Susanna, the Countess's maid. The Countess, chagrined, betrayed and disconcerted by her husband's philandering, joins with Susanna and Figaro in a plot to embarrass the Count; as such, she hopes he will change his ways and renew his devotion to her.

The Marriage of Figaro story deals with 18th century social struggles between lower class servants and their aristocratic masters, the intrigues in their relationships complicated by sex, rivalries, jealousies, betrayals and revenge.

Story Narrative with Music Highlights

Overture:

The Overture to *The Marriage of Figaro* captures the spirit of the opera: its themes are specific to the Overture and do not appear elsewhere in the opera.

Mozart musically suggests the story's underlying ironies and satire with bubbling and delightful motives; the music conveys a sense of rollicking good humor, but also contains subtle suggestions of the story's intrigues and skullduggery.

Presto

Presto

ACT I: A room in the Chateau assigned to Figaro and Susanna.

Figaro and his bride-to-be, Susanna, are making last minute preparations for their wedding. The Count has assigned them to new quarters and presented them with a new bed. Figaro is preoccupied with measuring how the bed will fit in the room, while Susanna tries on a hat she has made to wear at her wedding: the traditional wreath of orange blossoms, known as *le chapeau de mariage*. Susanna becomes irritated because Figaro takes no interest in her hat, but her petulance finally succeeds in getting his attention.

Intuitively, Susanna is suspicious of the Count's sudden generosity in which he provided them with a room extremely close to his own quarters. At the same time, she is exasperated by Figaro's unsuspecting complacency, and his failure to realize that the proximity of their rooms may indeed be an intentional ploy by the lustful Count. Susanna awakens Figaro's mistrust of the Count by convincing him that the Count does not really want her close to her mistress, the Countess. On the contrary, she concludes that he wants Susanna conveniently located so that he could invent an errand that would dispense with Figaro, and then have her at his mercy.

The Count has become a philanderer who is no longer satisfied with salacious amusement away from home. On the contrary, he has decided that he has many opportunities for amorous adventure right in his own chateau. Susanna has heard from Don Basilio that the Count has intentions of renewing the *droit de seigneur,* or *ius primae noctis,* the old custom of the feudal right of the lord, a tradition by which the lord of the manor, in compensation for the loss of one of his female servants through marriage, had the right to deflower his feudal dependents before the husband took possession. Susanna has become the Count's intended victim, and with his customary despicable arrogance, he intends to achieve with consent from Susanna, the right he ceded by law.

Upon hearing Susanna's revelation, Figaro becomes stunned and outraged. He is unable to comprehend how the Count could betray him after he provided his unstinting help and friendship during the Count's courting of Rosina. Figaro becomes alarmed, and is now convinced that the Count, if he succeeds in becoming the ambassador in London, will send him off as his courier, and then have Susanna alone as his prey.

Figaro decides that he must outwit his master, and with his customary confidence, concludes that the Count will never be able to match his ingenuity. In his aria, "Se vuol ballare, Signor Contino" ("If you want to dance my little Count"), Figaro sums up the underlying tension of their class struggle, a conflict in which the lower classes require cunning to survive under aristocratic power. Although Susanna is confident she can control the lascivious Count, Figaro is more apprehensive, and even somewhat jealous.

"Se vuol ballare, signor Contino"

Allegretto
FIGARO

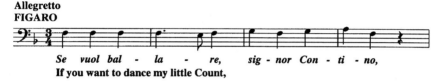

In a moment of desperation, Figaro borrowed money from Marcellina, Dr. Bartolo's housekeeper, however, lacking collateral, he haphazardly promised to marry her if he could not reimburse her. Marcellina arrives to demand repayment from Figaro, and with the encouragement and assistance of Dr. Bartolo, intends to legally force Figaro to marry her. Likewise, Dr. Bartolo seeks revenge against Figaro for his past trickery in helping the Count lure Rosina from him. And further gratifying Bartolo is the opportunity to rid himself of the now extremely unattractive Marcellina, who, many years earlier, was his mistress and the bearer of his illegitimate son.

Marcellina and Dr. Bartolo unite and become impassioned accomplices in their conspiracy against Figaro: Bartolo concludes that his hour of revenge against "that rascal Figaro" may have finally arrived, and he expresses his exhilaration in the traditional grand buffo style, his patter aria: "La vendetta, oh, la vendetta!" ("Vengeance, oh vengeance!")

"La vendetta, oh, la vendetta!"
Allegro con spirito
BARTOLO

When Susanna reappears, Marcellina provokes her into a rivalry for Figaro by planting seeds of jealousy. The two women argue with mock courtesies, sarcasm, and feigned sincerity and politeness. But Marcellina cannot restrain her spite and disdain; she insults Susanna by calling her "the Count's beautiful Susanna." Likewise, Susanna responds by insulting Marcellina's advancing age.

After Marcellina departs, Cherubino, the page of the chateau, arrives. He is an adolescent suffering from youthful erotic awakenings, and a pulse that uncontrollably races when he encounters the opposite sex: the ubiquitous page's hyperactive hormones seem to place him in all of the wrong places at the wrong time.

Yesterday, in particular, Cherubino aroused the Count's anger when the Count caught him in a rendezvous with Barbarina, the gardener Antonio's daughter. The Count became enraged; after all, Cherubino was in truth his rival for Barbarina. The Count angrily warned Cherubino, and the page fears his fury and that he would be expelled from the chateau. Cherubino begs Susanna to intercede with the Countess and ask her to dissuade the Count's agitation.

However, true to his uncontrollable passions, the young Cherubino reveals to Susanna that he has fallen deeply in love with no less a personage than the Countess herself, his godmother. Ecstatic and inspired by his love for the Countess, he expresses his erotic passions, sensibilities which he cannot understand and confuse him.

"Non so più cosa son, cosa faccio"

Allegro vivace
CHERUBINO

Non so   più   co - sa son,   co - sa   fac - cio,
I no longer know who I am, or what I do.

Suddenly, the new quarters of Susanna and Figaro are invaded by the Count himself. Cherubino, fearing the Count, particularly because he should not be in Susanna's quarters at all, hastily conceals himself behind a chair. The Count, believing that he is alone with Susanna, pleads for her love. He explains that he may receive an ambassadorship to London, and suggests to Susanna that his appointment would provide a magnificent opportunity for them to develop a relationship: of course, the unsuspecting Count's amorous proposition is overheard by the hiding Cherubino.

Approaching footsteps are heard. The Count, fearing a scandal if he is caught in Susanna's room, decides to hide behind the chair. Cherubino avoids him by scattering around and seating himself in the chair; Susanna covers the young page with her bridal dress.

Don Basilio arrives, the chateau's gossiping music master and ingenious fabricator of intrigues. He proceeds to make malicious —— yet accurate — insinuations about Cherubino's rapturous flirtations and amorous behavior toward the Countess. The Count, hiding behind the chair, overhears Basilio's blasphemous accusations about his wife, emerges from behind the chair, erupts into a towering rage, and demands details and an explanation from Basilio.

In fear, Basilio retracts his accusations by excusing them as mere suspicion. Nevertheless, the seeds of jealousy have been planted in the Count's mind. And, he is outraged that his rival is the young page Cherubino, a continuing obstacle to his pursuits.

The Count describes how yesterday, when he was in Barbarina's room, he drew away a table cloth, and discovered Cherubino hiding under a table. As he demonstrates the event, he sweeps aside Susanna's dress from the chair, and in shock, surprise, and exasperation, for the second time in a mere few days, he finds Cherubino again in a compromising situation. The Count becomes outraged; Susanna expresses horror; and Don Basilio erupts into malicious delight and laughter.

The Count concludes that Cherubino and Susanna are having a clandestine affair, which serves to further infuriate him: not only has Cherubino overheard his failed attempts to seduce Susanna, but the lad seems to have had more success with Susanna than he has had. The Count now realizes that he has an opportunity to avenge his cunning valet, so he sends Basilio to fetch Figaro so he can reveal his betrothed's infidelities.

Figaro arrives with a group of peasants, all ironically praising their magnanimous master: the man of virtue who abolished the ancient aristocratic privilege of *droit de signeur*. Likewise, Figaro joins the praise and requests that at their wedding the Count should place the wedding veil on Susanna's head to symbolize the bride's innocence because he has relinquished his former privilege.

The Count becomes thoroughly enraged with the omnipresent Cherubino. Susanna suggests that he forgive the innocent and naive lad. But the Count has a sudden inspiration, a contrivance to rid himself completely of Cherubino. The boy will receive an officer's commission in the Count's Seville regiment and must leave immediately. Now delirious and elated with the impending resolution to his problem with Cherubino, the Count and the malicious Don Basilio depart.

Cherubino shakes in dreaded fear as Figaro taunts him, painting a vivid picture of the glories and terrors of military life: now, instead of flirtation and tender love-making, Cherubino will embark on a military career and be subject to weary drills and marching.

"Non più andrai farfallone amoroso"

Vivace
FIGARO

Non più andrai, far - fallon - e a - mo - ro - so,
You'll no longer be fluttering around night and day,

Figaro exults in the idea of Cherubino's departure: like the Count, his life will certainly be sweeter without the menacing presence of this impetuous young page.

ACT II: The Countess's apartment

The Countess, alone with her thoughts, meditates about her happy past, and her unhappy present. She deeply loves her husband, but she has slowly realized that she is not the only woman in his life. The Countess, touchingly and expressively, expresses her distressed feelings, praying for relief from her grief, and ultimately, that her husband's affections may be restored to her.

"*Porgi amor, qualche ristoro*"
Larghetto
COUNTESS

Por - gi a - mor,   *qualche   ri - sto - ro,*
Cupid, love, relieve my pain and sorrows.

The Countess, despairing about the Count's wayward affections, joins with Susanna to invent a scheme that will serve to thwart the Count's amorous adventures. They decide to launch a plot to outwit him and teach him a lesson: they will expose his infidelities, ridicule and embarrass him. And by arousing his jealousy, they hope to persuade him to reawaken his love for the Countess and return to being a faithful husband.

Their intrigue involves the delivery to the Count of an anonymous letter which reveals that the Countess has made a rendezvous with a secret "lover." The resourceful Figaro will arrange to have Don Basilio deliver the letter to the Count. At the same time, Susanna will arrange a clandestine rendezvous with the Count, but Cherubino will be in her place, dressed in her clothes: after Figaro's description of military life, Cherubino will do anything to postpone his entry into the army.

Cherubino arrives, and is delighted and excited that he has been able to see the Countess before his departure. Susanna persuades him to entertain the Countess with a song he has written for her. Cherubino's romantic song praises the Countess, complementing her insight into the intrigues of love and romance.

"*Voi che sapete che cosa è amor*"

Andante
CHERUBINO

Voi,   che sa - pe - te   che   co - sa è amor,
You indeed know what love is,

The Countess sees Cherubino's commission and remarks in surprise that it lacks the official seal. Susanna proceeds to dress Cherubino in woman's clothes for the masquerade, but becomes frustrated by the impetuous youth who keeps turning his attention to the Countess.

"*Venite inginocchiatevi*"

Allegretto
SUSANNA

Ve - nite   in- gi - noc - chia-tevi,
Come, kneel down, and stay still.

Just as Cherubino's female disguise is completed, the Count is heard angrily knocking at the door. Cherubino, fearing another encounter with his master, immediately hides in an adjoining closet. The Count is agitated: he received the Countess's letter for a rendezvous with a secret lover and is now enraged by suspicions of her infidelity. And when he finds the Countess's door locked — an unprecedented action — his suspicions become further aroused.

The door is opened, and the Count immediately presents the letter to the Countess, fuming at her as he incriminates her infidelity. At the same time, the Count's suspicions are further aroused when he hears noises from an adjoining room — the hiding Cherubino of course. Nervously, the Countess tries to deter the Count, explaining that the noise is from Susanna who is dressing. But the Count is beside himself with jealousy, fears a scandal and the ridicule of a cuckolded husband. He suspects that the Countess's lover is hiding in the closet, and demands that Susanna — if it is indeed Susanna — come out of the room and allay his suspicions.

In desperation, the Count unsuccessfully tries to physically open the door. Thwarted in his attempts, he decides to secure tools to break down the door, but to avoid any skulduggery, he insists that the Countess leave with him. Both the Count and Countess depart, but beforehand, the Count locks the doors, in effect locking both Susanna and Cherubino inside.

After they have departed, Susanna fetches Cherubino. Cherubino is terrified and intimidated lest he should be discovered by the Count. With no other exit, Cherubino escapes through an open window, his jump witnessed by the inebriated Antonio, the gardener, who becomes puzzled and disconcerted at what he has just seen.

Susanna proceeds to hide herself in the adjoining closet and await the return of the Count and Countess. The Count arrives with an iron bar in hand, viciously intent to forcibly open the closet door. The Countess, unaware that Cherubino has escaped and that Susanna has replaced him in the closet, becomes anxious and nervous as she tries to deter him. She decides that she has no alternative but to confess to her husband that it is indeed the young Cherubino in the closet; at the same time she tries to persuade the Count that Cherubino is merely an innocent young lad who is unworthy of his anger.

Nevertheless, the Count is implacable; he is angry, inflamed with rage, and blind with jealousy, particularly after he received the letter revealing that the Countess planned a secret rendezvous with a lover. He disregards the Countess's anxious pleading, and becomes obsessed to learn the identity of the Countess's secret lover hiding in her closet.

"Esci or mai, garzon malnato"

Allegro
COUNT

E - sci o mai, garzon mal - na -to, scia - gu - ra - to, non tardar!
Come out now, uncouth lad, scoundrel, and don't delay!

Just as the Count is about to break down the door, and with his sword poised for the kill, the door opens. Susanna appears calmly at the threshold, her demeanor expressing wide-eyed innocence. The Count is dumbfounded, shocked and surprised that it was indeed Susanna in the room. The Countess is duly astonished but relieved by the resolution of a seemingly insoluble dilemma. In effect, Susanna's emergence has confirmed the Countess's original explanation that it was indeed Susanna dressing in the room. The Countess quickly clarifies her earlier confession to the Count, explaining that the reason she told him Cherubino was in the room was merely a ruse to inflame his jealousy: she knew all the time that Susanna was in the room. The Count becomes humiliated, senses that he has been duped, and refuses to believe that Susanna was alone in the dressing room. He decides to enter the room and investigate further. While he is gone, Susanna advises the confused Countess that Cherubino escaped by jumping from the window.

The Count returns, confused and embarrassed that his suspicions were unfounded. He becomes contrite, asks the Countess to forgive his behavior and confirms his love for her. Nevertheless, he reproaches the Countess for the cruelty of her foolish jokes. But the Countess is angry and unmerciful. She expresses her bitterness to the Count for his unfounded suspicion of her, and reminds him of his continuing neglect and indifference to her.

Nevertheless, jealousy has been implanted in the Count's mind. He still suspects that it was indeed Cherubino hiding in her room, and demands an explanation of the anonymous letter. The Countess explains that it was all part of a harmless joke perpetrated by Figaro to provoke and tease him. The Count again begs her forgiveness, and this time, she grants it.

Excitedly, Figaro arrives to announces that the musicians have assembled, all the arrangements are in place, and their wedding can proceed. The Count is wary and suspicious of Figaro, and seizes the opportunity to question him about the infamous letter. The resourceful Figaro vigorously denies any knowledge of it, but his memory is sharpened by whispers from Susanna and the Countess; then Figaro admits to the Count that he was the writer of the letter.

Antonio arrives to further confound Figaro and present him with new problems. In a comically inebriated state, Antonio complains that someone jumped out of the window of the Countess's room, trampled his flowers, and broke a flower pot. Figaro quickly admits that he was the culprit, and even shows them that he injured his leg in the process.

That being the case, Antonio confronts Figaro with a paper that he dropped in the garden during his jump: Cherubino's officer's commission. The Count senses chicanery. He grabs the paper from Antonio, and then interrogates Figaro, asking him to explain the contents of the paper. The Countess recognizes the paper, whispers to Susanna that it is Cherubino's commission, and Susanna in turn whispers its content to Figaro. Figaro, now prompted by the women, reveals to the Count that the paper is Cherubino's commission.

The Count inquires why the commission was in Figaro's possession, and again, the Countess prompts the answer through Susanna's subtle whispers. With great confidence, Figaro vindicates himself and announces that Cherubino gave him the commission to secure its missing seal.

Figaro now faces his most serious crisis. The malicious trio of Marcellina, Dr. Bartolo, and Don Basilio burst in and demand justice. Specifically, Figaro must honor his promise to repay Marcellina's loan to him, and if he cannot, he is legally bound to marry her. The Count becomes ecstatic: he now has found a means to avenge his wily valet; after all, with Figaro out of the way, he would have no obstacle in pursuing Susanna.

The Count announces that he will act as magistrate and adjudicate Marcellina's claim; it will be a biased decision that will enable the eager Count to settle accounts with his troublesome valet. The Count again postpones the marriage between Figaro and Susanna until all of the complications between servants and masters are resolved.

ACT III: A hall inCount Almaviva's chateau

Count Almaviva eagerly seals Cherubino's army commission, thus ridding himself of this vexatious youthful rival for his wife's affections, as well as the other women he has been pursuing in the chateau. He reflects on the senselessness of strange recent events, remaining perplexed and suspicious. He refuses to accept or believe Figaro's explanations, so he still wonders: Who jumped from the balcony? Who is the Countess's lover? Who wrote the anonymous letter?

Susanna approaches the Count. The lustful Count anxiously complains that he has become tormented by his desire for her. He suggests that they meet secretly, providing Susanna with a perfect opportunity to pursue the scheme to embarrass the Count: Susanna agrees to meet the Count for a tryst in the garden that evening after her wedding. The impatient Count becomes elated. In his triumph, he will finally have his moment to seduce Susanna, and at the same time, his revenge against Figaro.

"Crudel! Perchè finora farmi languir così?"

Cru - del! Perchè fi - no - ra far — mi languir co - sì?
Cruel one! Why did you make me languish like this until now?

But in truth, Susanna's agreement for a secret rendezvous will enable the Countess to teach her husband a lesson for his philandering: her plan is that the Count will be meeting the Countess herself, deceiving him because she will be dressed in Susanna's clothes.

As Susanna departs, she runs into Figaro who is on his way to the hearing of Marcellina's suit against him. Susanna tells Figaro that his case has been won, and she has the money to pay Marcellina. (Neither Figaro nor the Count know that Susanna borrowed money from the Countess to pay back Marcellina.)

The Count overhears Figaro and Susanna. He becomes vindictive and explodes in rage and condemnation: the frustrated Count concludes that Figaro, a mere servant, seems to have been born to torment him and laugh at his misfortune. Nevertheless, the Count is comforted by hopes for revenge against his vexatious valet.

The Count presides over his court to determine Figaro's obligations to Marcellina. The stuttering lawyer, Don Curzio, alleges that if Figaro does not reimburse Marcellina, he is obliged to marry her. Figaro ingeniously engineers a solution to his crisis: he claims that because he is of noble birth, he cannot marry without the consent of his parents; he is ignorant of his parentage, but hopes to find them some day. To prove his claim of noble birth, he reveals a branded spatula mark on his arm. Marcellina recognizes the mark, and to everybody's amazement, announces that Figaro is her long-lost son: the fruit of an early love affair between Marcellina and Dr. Bartolo. Raging impotently, the Count watches in vain as Figaro and his new-found parents reunite and embrace in celebration.

Susanna arrives with money to settle Figaro's debts. She observes Marcellina bestowing kisses on Figaro, but is unaware of the reason for the celebration that she is witnessing. She turns into a jealous rage, and proceeds to box Figaro on his ear before he gets a chance to explain his unexpected change of fortune.

Nevertheless, Susanna is quickly told the truth, and the new family erupts into a spirited celebration. Dr. Bartolo announces that he will marry Marcellina forthwith, Figaro is heaped with gifts, Marcellina gives her long-lost son his promissory note as his wedding present, and Dr. Bartolo, ironically Figaro's father, hands him a purse of money. Susanna embraces her future parents-in-law, and all signs point to the four of them celebrating a double wedding: finally, all obstacles to the marriage of Susanna and Figaro seem to have been eliminated.

In a short scene, Cherubino is with Barbarina. It is obvious that the young page has not followed his orders and left for his regiment in Seville. They decide that they will disguise Cherubino in peasant girl's clothes so he can remain for the wedding festivities.

The Countess is deeply concerned about how her husband will react when he eventually learns of their intrigue. She deeply loves the Count, and indeed wants to punish him for his amorous excesses. Nevertheless, she deplores the fact that she must seek help from her servants to win back her husband's affection: a plot in which she has to exchange clothes with her maid Susanna. (The original scheme to disguise Cherubino as Susanna has been dropped.) Sadly, she recalls the days of her former happiness, and clings to her hopes that the Count will renew his devotion to her.

In a moment of tenderness and beauty, the brokenhearted Countess laments those lost days of happiness and bliss. Yet, she has not become embittered, and bears no malice toward the Count, although he has obviously been duplicitous since the moment they married. Nevertheless, she is forgiving, expresses hope, and yearns to restore her past happiness.

"Dove sono i bei momenti"

Andantino
COUNTESS

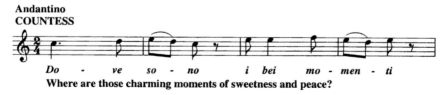

Do - ve so - no i bei mo - men - ti
Where are those charming moments of sweetness and peace?

The Countess dictates a letter which Susanna writes down. The intriguing note is directed to the Count, and fixes the exact time and place for the evening rendezvous: the Count is to meet Susanna in the garden: "under the pines where the gentle zephyrs blow." Of course, he will not be meeting Susanna, but rather, the Countess dressed in Susanna's clothes. The note is sealed with a brooch pin, and the Count must return the pin as confirmation of his understanding and agreement to keep the appointment.

Just before the wedding ceremony, village peasant girls arrive with flowers for the Countess. Cherubino is dressed as a peasant girl. Antonio arrives holding Cherubino's hat. He notices that one of the girls is none other than Cherubino in disguise, reveals his identity and proceeds to place the hat on his head.

The Count is about to explode in outrage. But Barbarina, deeply in love with Cherubino, comes to the page's rescue. In a declaration that virtually embarrasses the Count, she reminds him that during those many moments when he wanted to kiss her, he promised that he would grant her any wish; and she tells the Count that her wish now is to have Cherubino as her husband. The Count, again facing a perplexing crisis, wonders whether demons have overcome his destiny.

Figaro arrives, and the irritated and agitated Count asks him again who it was who jumped out of the window the other morning. But the tension of the moment is inadvertently broken as musicians start playing the wedding march: finally, the moment for the wedding of Figaro and Susanna has arrived.

The Count presides over the double wedding ceremony of Susanna and Figaro and Marcellina and Dr. Bartolo. The Count, while muttering words of revenge against Figaro, places the wedding veil on Susanna. As Susanna kneels before the Count, she slips him a note: the invitation to meet her in the garden that evening. Figaro, unaware of the Countess's new scheme, watches the Count open the note and prick his finger on the brooch pin. Figaro rightly suspects that a clandestine love intrigue is afoot, but he does not imagine that his beloved Susanna is involved. The Count, in anticipation of his rendezvous, hurriedly ends the ceremony, and promises further celebrations that evening.

ACT IV: _The garden of the chateau_

The Count gave Barbarina the brooch to return to its sender and confirm the rendezvous. To her consternation and distress, Barbarina lost the pin. While she searches in the evening darkness, Figaro arrives and helps the unsuspecting Barbarina look for the pin, and she disingenuously reveals the contents of the note, and the planned rendezvous of the Count and Susanna.

Figaro, who was not privy to this new phase of the Countess-Susanna charade, jumps to the conclusion that his new bride, Susanna, is faithless and intends to yield to the Count this very evening. Inflamed with passions of jealousy and betrayal, Figaro invites his new parents, Dr. Bartolo and Marcellina, to join him and witness his new wife's infidelity and faithlessness.

Nevertheless, Marcellina defends the constancy and fortitude of womanhood, and refuses to believe that Susanna would deceive Figaro. But in his anger and despair, Figaro believes he is the victim of deception, and warns all men to open their eyes to the fickleness of women: Figaro believes he has become a cuckold on the very first night of his marriage.

"Aprite un po' quegl'occhi, uomini incauti a schiocchi"

Moderato
FIGARO

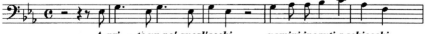

A-pri - te un po' quegl'occhi,   uomini incauti a schiocchi,
Open your eyes little, imprudent and foolish men,

Susanna and the Countess arrive, each wearing the other's clothes. Figaro hides himself in the expectation of catching Susanna and the Count *in flagrante*.

Susanna, advised by Marcellina, knows that Figaro is spying nearby, decides to teach her mistrusting new husband a lesson. With poignancy, she addresses a song to the supposed lover whom she awaits, telling him how she anticipates this night of love. Figaro, aroused and inflamed, hears Susanna but cannot see her in the dark: he does not know that it is he, not the Count, who is the subject of her amorous reflections.

"Deh viene, non tardar, o gioja bella"

Andante
SUSANNA

Deh vie - ni, non tar - dar,   o gio - ja bel - la,
Come, don't be late, my heart's delight,

The final scene is saturated with complications, confusion, and mistaken identities. Cherubino arrives, starts to make love to the Countess, thinking, from the clothes she wears, that she is Susanna. Suddenly, the Count arrives, steps between them, and in the dark and confusion, mistakenly receives a kiss from Cherubino. Now enraged, the Count aims a blow to Cherubino's ears, but instead, catches the hovering Figaro. The Count is left alone with whom he believes is Susanna, and proceeds to plead for her love and embraces, little knowing that the woman he is attempting to seduce is his own wife, the Countess.

Figaro wanders about, finds whom he believes is the Countess, and suggests that they together catch the Count with Susanna. But the Countess (Susanna) forgets herself for a moment and fails to disguise her voice. Figaro intuitively grasps the situation perfectly, and his jealousy instantly evaporates.

Nevertheless, Figaro seeks revenge. Theatrically, he begins to declare his passionate love for the dressed as the Countess, which, in turn, infuriates Susanna, rouses her jealousy, and prompts her to rain blows on Figaro. Their argument ends with the newlywed's first loving reconciliation.

Then Figaro and Susanna enact an impassioned moment of love while the Count looks on. He becomes irate when he sees Figaro and his wife, but the Count, true to character, has more important priorities: he leaves the scene en route for his rendezvous with Susanna.

The Countess, now dressed in her own clothes, makes a dignified appearance, and clears up the chaos and confusion by advising everyone to cease their foolish games. Figaro, Susanna, and finally the Countess, explain the charade and open the Count's eyes. He has been caught *in flagrante* with his own wife, and realizing that he has been outwitted, there is nothing he can do but acknowledge his folly with good grace. In a complete change of mood and heart, the Count begs the Countess's forgiveness which she lovingly grants.

All the crises seem to have been resolved and reconciled: there is cause for celebration to begin in earnest as all the lovers are reunited.

Beaumarchais's "Crazy Day" ends, saved for posterity with Mozart's impeccable musical characterizations.

THE MARRIAGE OF FIGARO

Libretto

OVERTURE

Presto

Presto

ACT I

A partly-furnished room, with a large chair in the center.
Figaro measures the floor while Susanna tries on a hat before a mirror.

FIGARO:
Cinque... dieci.... venti... trenta...
trentasei...quarantatre

SUSANNA:
Ora sì ch'io son contenta;
sembra fatto inver per me.
Guarda un po', mio caro Figaro,
guarda adesso il mio cappello.

FIGARO:
Sì mio core, or è più bello,
sembra fatto inver per te.

SUSANNA e FIGARO:
Ah, il mattino alle nozze vicino
quanto è dolce al (mio/tuo) tenero sposo.

SUSANNA:
Questo bel cappellino vezzoso
che Susanna ella stessa si fe!

Cosa stai misurando, caro il mio Figaretto?

FIGARO:
Io guardo se quel letto che ci destina il Conte
farà buona figura in questo loco.

FIGARO: *(measuring)*
Five....ten....twenty....thirty....
thirty-six.....forty-three.

SUSANNA: *(looking in the mirror)*
Now I indeed feel content.
It seems like it is made for me.
Look at me, my dear Figaro,
Look at this hat of mine right now.

FIGARO:
Yes my love, it is very pretty.
It seems like it was truly made for you.

SUSANNA and FIGARO:
Oh, your/my tender love is so welcome on this
wedding morning.

SUSANNA:
I made this pretty and charming little hat
all by myself!

What are you measuring, my dear little Figaro?

FIGARO:
I'm checking whether that bed the Count
ordered for us will fit well here.

SUSANNA:
E in questa stanza?

FIGARO:
Certo: a noi la cede generoso il padrone.

SUSANNA:
Io per me te la dono.

FIGARO:
E la ragione?

SUSANNA:
La ragione l'ho qui.

FIGARO:
Io non capisco perchè tanto ti spiace la più
comoda stanza del palazzo.

SUSANNA:
Perch'io son la Susanna, e tu sei pazzo.

FIGARO:
Grazie; non tanti elogi! Guarda un poco
se potriasi star meglio in altro loco.

FIGARO:
Se a caso madama la notte ti chiama,
din din; in due passi da quella puoi gir.
Vien poi l'occasione che vuolmi il
padrone,don, don; in tre salti lo vado a servir.

SUSANNA:
Così se il mattino il caro Contino,
din din; e ti manda tre miglia lontan,
don don; a mia porta il diavol lo porta,
ed ecco in tre salti....

FIGARO:
Susanna, pian, pian.

SUSANNA:
Ascolta

FIGARO:
Fa presto.

SUSANNA:
Se udir brami il resto, discaccia i sospetti
che torto mi fan.

SUSANNA:
In this room?

FIGARO:
Certainly! Our generous master gave it to us.

SUSANNA:
I don't like his gift.

FIGARO:
For what reason?

SUSANNA: *(touching her forehead)*
I have the reason here.

FIGARO:
I don't understand why you're unhappy with the
most convenient room in the palace?

SUSANNA:
Because I am Susanna, and you are crazy.

FIGARO:
Thanks for the compliments!
See if you can find a better place for it.

FIGARO:
If Madame should call you in the evening — ding,
ding — you can be there in two steps.
If the occasion arises that the master calls me —
don, don — I can be at his service in three jumps.

SUSANNA: *(ironically)*
If in the morning the dear Count commands
you three miles away,
the devil appears at my door, and then in three
jumps....

FIGARO:
Susanna, softly, softly.

SUSANNA:
Listen.

FIGARO:
Hurry.

SUSANNA:
If you want to hear the rest, drive away
your suspicions for they hurt me.

FIGARO:
Udir bramo il resto, i dubbi, i sospetti
gelare mi fan.

SUSANNA:
Or bene; ascolta, e taci!

FIGARO:
Parla: che c'è di nuovo?

SUSANNA:
Il signor Conte, stanco di andar cacciando le
straniere bellezze forestiere, vuole ancor nel
castello ritentar la sua sorte, né già di sua
consorte, bada bene, appetito gli viene

FIGARO:
E di chi dunque?

SUSANNA:
Della tua Susanetta.

FIGARO:
Di te?

SUSANNA:
Di me medesma. E tu credevi, che fosse la mia
dote metto del tuo bel viso?

FIGARO:
Me n'ero lusingato.

FIGARO:
Chi suona! La Contessa?

SUSANNA:
Addio, addio, Figaro bello.

FIGARO:
Coraggio, mio tesoro.

SUSANNA:
E tu, cervello.

FIGARO:
I want to hear the rest. These doubts and
suspicions make my blood chill.

SUSANNA:
Well listen and be quiet!

FIGARO:
Then speak. What's the matter?

SUSANNA:
The Count has tired of chasing foreign beauties,
and he again wants to try his chances in the castle.
He's already tired of his wife, and his appetite is
for other women.

FIGARO:
And who is it then?

SUSANNA:
Your dear little Susanna.

FIGARO:
You?

SUSANNA:
Me! And you thought that my charms were
only for your eyes?

FIGARO:
I've flattered myself.

(a bell rings)
FIGARO:
Who rings, the Countess?

SUSANNA:
Farewell, farewell, handsome Figaro.

FIGARO:
Courage my treasure.

SUSANNA:
And you use your head!

Susanna kisses Figaro, and then she departs.

FIGARO:
Bravo,signor padrone! Ora incomincio
a capir il mistero, e a veder schietto
tutto il vostro progetto: a Londra è vero?

FIGARO:
Bravo, my lord! Now I begin to understand the
mystery, and I clearly see all of your schemes.
Really, to London?

Voi ministro, io corriero, e la Susanna secreta ambasciatrice.	You'll be a minister, I a messenger, and Susanna a secret ambassador.
Non sarà, non sarà. Figaro il dice.	It won't happen. Figaro says so.

Allegretto
FIGARO

Se   vuol bal - la - re,   sig - nor Con - ti - no,

Se vuol ballare Signor Contino, il chitarrino le suonerò.	If you want to dance, Mr. Count, my guitar will accompany you.
Se vuol venire nella mia scuola la capriola le insegnerò.	If you want to learn how to play tricks, come to my school.
Saprò, ma piano, meglio ogni arcano dissimulando scoprir potrò!	Little by little, I'll learn and discover your every mystery and intrigue!
L'arte schermendo, l'arte adoprando, di qua pungendo, di là scherzando, tutte le macchine rovescerò.	And when I know, I become the master of self-protection, the art of ingenuity, fighting here, and joking there.
Se vuol ballare Signor Contino, il chitarrino le suonerò.	If you want to dance, my Count, my guitar will accompany you.

Figaro departs.

Dr. Bartolo enters with Marcellina, who holds a contract in her hand.

BARTOLO:
Ed aspettaste il giorno fissato a le sue nozze
per parlarmi di questo?

BARTOLO:
And you waited until their wedding day to tell
me about this?

MARCELLINA:
Io non mi perdo, dottor mio, di coraggio:
per romper de' sponsali più avanzati di
questo.Bastò spesso un pretesto, ed egli ha meco,
oltre questo contratto, certi impegni, so io, basta,
convien la Susanna atterrir.

MARCELLINA:
My dear doctor, I did not lose my courage to
break off the match earlier. He has other
agreements with me, so a mere pretext would
be enough.
Summon Susanna and terrify her.

Convien con arte impuntigliarli a rifiutar il
Conte. Egli per vendicarsi prenderà il mio
partito, e Figaro così fia mio marito.

Insist that she subtly refuse the Count. The
Count will take my side, seek revenge, and
Figaro will become my husband.

BARTOLO:
Bene, io tutto farò: senza riserve tutto a me palesate.
(Avrei pur gusto di dar per moglie la mia serva antica a chi mi fece un dì rapir l'amica.)

BARTOLO: *(takes the contract from her)*
All right. I'll do it for you, but don't hide anything, and let me know everything.
(Figaro made me lose my love, so I'll have my revenge by giving him my old servant.)

Allegro con spirito
BARTOLO

La   ven - det - ta,   oh,   la   ven-det - ta!

La vendetta, oh, la vendetta!
È un piacer serbato ai saggi.
L'obliar l'onte e gli oltraggi è bassezza, è ognor viltà.

Vengeance, oh vengeance!
It is the pleasure of the wise.
It is cowardly and vile to forget affronts and insults.

Con l'astuzia, coll'arguzia, col giudizio, col criterio, si potrebbe, il fatto è serio!

One can achieve revenge with astuteness, cleverness, good sense and good judgment.

Ma credete si farà se tutto il codice dovessi volgere, se tutto l'indice dovessi leggere, con un equivoco, con un sinonimo qualche garbuglio si troverà. Tutta Siviglia conosce Bartolo: il birbo Figaro vostro sarà.

I'll address every aspect of the law and turn it to our benefit: I must read all the cases, find a loophole, a synonym, or a mistake.
All Seville knows Bartolo: he'll defeat that scoundrel Figaro.

Bartolo exits.

Susanna enters, carrying a night-cap, a ribbon, and a dressing gown.

MARCELLINA:
Tutto ancor non ho perso: mi resta la speranza.
Ma Susanna si avanza: io vo' provarmi.
Fingiam di non vederla.
E quella buona perla la vorrebbe sposar!

MARCELLINA:
I haven't lost yet. I still have hopes left.
But here comes Susanna. Let me begin.
I'll pretend not to see her.
And that's the pearl he wants to marry!

SUSANNA:
(Di me favella.)

SUSANNA:
(She's speaking about me.)

MARCELLINA:
Ma da Figaro alfine non può meglio sperarsi:
"l'argent fait tout."

MARCELLINA:
You can't expect anything else from Figaro, because money means everything to him!

SUSANNA:
(Che lingua! Manco male ch'ognun sa quanto vale.)

SUSANNA:
(What a tongue! Fortunately no one listens to what she says.)

MARCELLINA:
Brava! Questo è giudizio!
Con quegli occhi modesti, con quell'aria
pietosa, e poi....

SUSANNA:
Meglio è partir.

MARCELLINA:
Che cara sposa!

MARCELLINA:
Wonderful! That is sensible!
With those modest eyes, with that merciful
look, and then....

SUSANNA:
I had better go.

MARCELLINA:
What a charming bride!

With irony, both watch each other to see who will leave first.

Via resti servita, Madama brillante.

SUSANNA:
Non sono sì ardita, madama piccante.

MARCELLINA:
No, prima a lei tocca.

SUSANNA:
No, no, tocca a lei.

SUSANNA e MARCELLINA:
Io so i dover miei, non fo inciviltà.

MARCELLINA:
La sposa novella!
Del Conte la bella!
I meriti, il posto.
Per Bacco! Precipito se ancor resto quà.

SUSANNA:
La dama d'onore!
Di Spagna l'amore!
Stimabile età!
Sibilla decrepita,
da rider mi fa!

Do go first, grand lady.

SUSANNA: *(reverently)*
I'm not so bold, zesty lady.

MARCELLINA:
No. you go first.

SUSANNA:
No, no, first you.

SUSANNA and MARCELLINA:
I know good breeding and I'm never uncivil.

MARCELLINA:
This new bride!
The Count's choice!
The worth, the station.
By Bacchus, I'll lose if I stay here.

SUSANNA:
The lady of honor!
The love of Spain!
Respectable age!
Decrepit stutterer,
who makes me laugh!

Marcellina departs.

SUSANNA:
Va' là, vecchia pedante,
dottoressa arrogante,
perché hai letti due libri
e seccata madama in gioventù.

SUSANNA:
Go along, old pedant,
arrogant know-it-all.
Just because you read two books you pretend to
be a mature woman.

Cherubino enters.

CHERUBINO:
Susanetta, sei tu?

CHERUBINO:
Is that you, little Susanna?

SUSANNA:
Son io, cosa volete?

SUSANNA:
It's me. What do you want?

CHERUBINO:
Ah, cor mio, che accidente!

CHERUBINO:
Oh, dear one! What an accident!

SUSANNA:
Cor vostro! Cosa avvenne?

SUSANNA:
Sweetheart, what has happened?

CHERUBINO:
Il Conte ieri perché trovommi sol con
Barbarina, il congedo mi diede;
e se la Contessina, la mia bella comare,
grazia non m'intercede, io vado via,
io non ti vedo più, Susanna mia!

CHERUBINO:
Yesterday the Count found me alone with
Barbarina and dismissed me. If the Countess, my
beautiful godmother, is not kind and doesn't
intercede for me, I'll have to go away and
never see you again, my Susanna!

SUSANNA:
Non vedete più me! Bravo!
Ma dunque non più per la Contessa
secretamente il vostro cor sospira?

SUSANNA:
You won't see me any more! Great!
But you also won't be able to secretly pine for
the Countess?

CHERUBINO:
Ah, che troppo rispetto ella m'ispira!
Felice te, che puoi vederla quando vuoi,
che la vesti il mattino, che la sera la spogli, che
le metti gli spilloni, i merletti.

Cos'hai lì? Dimmi un poco.

CHERUBINO: *(sighing)*
Oh, she inspires so much respect from me!
You are fortunate because you can see her
whenever you want: dress her in the
morning, undress her in the evening,,
place her garments, needles, lace.
Tell me what you have there?

SUSANNA:
Ah, il vago nastro della notturna cuffia
di comare sì bella.

SUSANNA:
Oh, it's the ribbon belonging to your beautiful
godmother's nightcap.

CHERUBINO:
Deh, dammelo sorella, dammelo per pietà!

CHERUBINO:
Oh, for mercy's sake, give it to me!
(snatches the ribbon from Susanna)

SUSANNA:
Presto quel nastro!

SUSANNA:
Give me back that ribbon!

CHERUBINO:
O caro, o bello, o fortunato nastro!
Io non te'l renderò che colla vita!

CHERUBINO: *(admiring the ribbon)*
Oh dear, oh beautiful, oh fortunate ribbon!
In my lifetime I won't return it to you!

SUSANNA:
Cos'è quest'insolenza?

SUSANNA:
What is this impudence?

CHERUBINO:
Eh via, sta cheta!In ricompensa poi questa mia
canzonetta io ti vo' dare.

CHERUBINO:
Come now, don't be so angry!
In exchange, I want to give you my little song.

SUSANNA:
E che ne debbo fare?

SUSANNA:
And what am I to do with it?

CHERUBINO:
Leggila alla padrona, leggila tu medesma;
leggila a Barbarina, a Marcellina;
leggila ad ogni donna del palazzo!

CHERUBINO:
Read it to my lady, read it to yourself, read it
to Barbarina, to Marcellina,
read it to every women in the palace!

SUSANNA:
Povero Cherubin, siete voi pazzo!

SUSANNA:
Poor Cherubino, you have gone mad?

Allegro vivace

CHERUBINO:
Non so più cosa son, cosa faccio,
or di foco, ora sono di ghiaccio,
ogni donna cangiar di colore,
ogni donna mi fa palpitar.

CHERUBINO:
I no longer know who I am, or what I do.
I'm all fire, then I'm all ice.
Every woman makes me blush.
Every woman makes me throb.

Solo ai nomi d'amor, di diletto,
mi si turba, mi s'altera il petto
e a parlare mi sforza d'amore
un desio ch'io non posso spiegar.

It is merely the mention of love, of delight, that
disturbs me and unsettles my heart. The power
of love has become a desire that I can't
explain.

Parlo d'amor vegliando,
parlo d'amor sognando,
all'acque, all'ombre, ai monti,
ai fiori, all'erbe, ai fonti,
all'eco, all'aria, ai venti,
che il suon de' vani accenti
portano via con sé.
E se non ho chi mi oda,
parlo d'amor con me.

I speak of love while awake,
I speak of love while I sleep,
to water, to shadows, to mountains,
to flowers, to herbs, to fountains,
to the echo, to the air, to the wind.
The sounds of my hopeless laments carry me
away.
And if no one hears me,
I speak of love to myself.

The Count is heard coming.

SUSANNA:
Taci, vien gente, il Conte!
Oh, me meschina!

SUSANNA:
Quiet, someone's coming. It's the Count. He
shouldn't find you here!

In fear, Cherubino hides behind a chair.

IL CONTE:
Susanna, mi sembri agitata e confusa.

COUNT:
Susanna, you seem agitated and confused.

SUSANNA:
Signor, io chiedo scusa,.
ma, se mai, qui sorpresa,..
per carità. Partite!

SUSANNA:
Sir. I beg your pardon.
But I'm just so surprised.
For mercy's sake, go!

IL CONTE:
Un momento, e ti lascio, odi.

COUNT: *(sits on the chair)*
One moment and then I'll leave. Listen.

SUSANNA:
Non odo nulla.

SUSANNA:
I will hear nothing.

IL CONTE:
Due parole. Tu sai che ambasciatore a Londra
il re mi dichiarò; di condur meco
Figaro destinai.

COUNT:
Just two words. You know that the King has
named me ambassador to London.
I intend to take Figaro with me.

SUSANNA:
Signor, se osassi...

SUSANNA:
Sir, I beg you...

IL CONTE:
Parla, parla, mia cara, e con quell dritto
ch'oggi prendi su me finché tu vivi
chiedi, imponi, prescrivi.

COUNT:
Talk to me, my dear. With the power that you
now have over me, you can ask, order, or
command anything.

SUSANNA:
Lasciatemi signor; dritti non prendo,
non ne vo', non ne intendo.
Oh me infelice!

SUSANNA:
Leave me, sir. I have no rights, nor wish or
propose any.
Oh I'm so unhappy!

IL CONTE:
Ah no, Susanna, io ti vo' far felice!
Tu ben sai quanto io t'amo: a te Basilio
tutto già disse.
Or senti, se per pochi momenti meco in giardin
sull'imbrunir del giorno.
Ah, per questo favore io pagherei.

COUNT:
No, Susanna. I want to make you happy!
You know well how much I love you. Basilio
has already told you.
Then listen, meet me tonight in the garden.
You know I'd pay for that favor.

BASILIO:
È uscito poco fa.

BASILIO: *(from outside)*
He not been gone for long.

IL CONTE:
Chi parla?

COUNT:
Who speaks?

SUSANNA:
Oh Dei!

SUSANNA:
Oh Gods!

IL CONTE:
Esci, e alcun non entri.

COUNT:
Go, and don't let anyone in.

SUSANNA:
Ch'io vi lasci qui solo?

SUSANNA:
That I'll leave you here alone?

BASILIO:
Da madama ei sarà, vado a cercarlo.

BASILIO:
Perhaps he is with my Lady. I'll go look for him.

IL CONTE:
Qui dietro mi porrò.

COUNT: *(pointing to the chair)*
I'll put myself behind this chair.

SUSANNA:
Non vi celate.

SUSANNA:
Don't hide.

IL CONTE
Taci, e cerca ch'ei parta.

COUNT:
Quiet. Try to get rid of him.

SUSANNA
Oimè! Che fate?

SUSANNA:
Oh my, what are you doing?

The Count conceals himself behind the large chair. Susanna places herself resourcefully before him, making signs to Cherubino to move. Cherubino avoids the Count by crawling around the chair.

BASILIO:
Susanna, il ciel vi salvi. Avreste a caso veduto il Conte?

BASILIO: *(from outside)*
Susanna, heavens save you. Have you by any chance seen the Count?

SUSANNA:
E cosa deve far meco il Conte?
Animo, uscite.

SUSANNA: *(annoyed)*
And what would the Count be doing with me? Get out, mindless one.

IL CONTE:
Chi parla?

COUNT:
Who's speaking?

SUSANNA:
O Dei!

SUSANNA:
Oh heavens!

IL CONTE:
Esci, ed alcun non entri.

COUNT:
You go. Don't let him come in.

SUSANNA:
Ch'io vi lasci qui solo?

SUSANNA:
And leave you here alone?

BASILIO:
Da madama sarà, vado a cercarlo.

BASILIO:
With my lady perhaps? I'll ask Susanna.

IL CONTE:
Qui dietro mi porrò.

COUNT:
I'll hide behind the chair.

SUSANNA:
Non vi celate.

SUSANNA:
No don't hide.

IL CONTE:
Taci, e cerca, ch'ei parta.

COUNT:
Quiet, and don't let him come in.

SUSANNA:
Ohime! Che fate!

SUSANNA:
Oh my! What should I do!

As the Count hides behind the chair, Cherubino scrambles around and sits in it.
Susanna covers him with a dress. Basilio enters.

BASILIO:
Susanna, il ciel vi salvi! Avreste caso veduto il Conte?

BASILIO:
Susanna, peace be with you! Have you seen the Count?

SUSANNA:
E cosa deve far meco il Conte? Animo, uscite.

SUSANNA:
What should I know about the Count? Pray, go away.

BASILIO:
Aspetate, sentite, Figaro di lui cerca.

BASILIO:
Wait, listen. Figaro is looking for him.

SUSANNA:
(Oh Cielo! Ei cerca chi, dopo voi, più l'odia.)

SUSANNA:
(Oh Heavens! He'll find the man who hates him most right here.)

IL CONTE:
(Vediam come mi serve.)

COUNT:
(Let's see how she serves me?)

BASILIO:
Io non ho mai nella moral sentito, ch'uno ch'ami la moglie odiii il marito. Per dir che il Conte v'ama.....

BASILIO:
I've never heard in the moral code that one who loves the wife hates the husband. To say that the Count loves you.....

SUSANNA
Sortite, vil ministro dell'altrui sfrenatezza: Io non ho d'uopo della vostra morale, del Conte, del suo amor.

SUSANNA:
You vile minister. How dare you make those suggestions! I refuse to talk about the Count's passions and desires.

BASILIO:
Non c'è alcun male.
Ha ciascun i suoi gusti: io mi credea che preferir dovreste per amante, come fan tutte quante, un signor liberal, prudente, e saggio, a un giovinastro, a un paggio.

BASILIO:
There's no harm done. It's a matter of taste. Yet I would imagine that you're like any other woman, and would choose for your lover a man who is rich, noble and quite discreet, instead of yielding to a page.

SUSANNA:
A Cherubino!

SUSANNA:
To Cherubino!

BASILIO:
A Cherubino! A Cherubin d'amore ch'oggi sul far del giorno passeggiava qui d'intorno, per entrar.

BASILIO:
Yes Cherubino! The love-child who hovers about here every morning, and passes in and out.

SUSANNA:
Uom maligno, un impostura è questa.

BASILIO:
È un maligno con voi chi ha gli occhi in testa?
E quella canzonetta?
Ditemi in confidenza; io sono amico,
ed altrui nulla dico;
è per voi, per madama?

SUSANNA:
(Chi diavol gliel'ha detto?)

BASILIO:
A proposito, figlia, instruitelo meglio;egli la
guarda a tavola sì spesso, e con tale
immodestia, che se il Conte s'accorge che su
tal punto sapete, egli è una bestia.

SUSANNA
Scellerato! E perché andate voi
tai menzogne spargendo?

BASILIO:
Io? Che ingiustizia! Quel che compro io vendo,
a quel che tutti dicono io non aggiungo un pelo.

IL CONTE:
Come, che dicon tutti?

BASILIO:
Oh bella!

SUSANNA:
Oh cielo!

SUSANNA:
Wicked man. This is slander.

BASILIO:
Is it wicked for one to have eyes in one's head?
And that song?
Tell me in confidence. I'm a friend and I speak
truths.
Was it for you, or was it for Madame?

SUSANNA:
(Who was the devil who told this to him?)

BASILIO:
By the way, my dear, tell Cherubino to be more
careful. He gloats at Madame with such
impudence, that if the Count would notice, you
well know, he'll become a savage.

SUSANNA:
You scoundrel! Why do you go about
spreading such lies?

BASILIO:
I? What injustice! I only say what I see, and
add not one iota to what everybody says.

COUNT: *(rises but troubled)*
What! What are they all saying!

BASILIO: *(aside)*
Oh beautiful one!

SUSANNA: *(aside)*
Oh Heavens!

The Count emerges from behind the chair.

IL CONTE:
Cosa sento! Tosto andate,
e scacciate il seduttor.

BASILIO:
(In qual punto son qui giunto!)
Perdonate, oh mio signor.

SUSANNA:
Che ruina, me meschina,
son oppressa dal dolor.

COUNT: *(to Basilio)*
What do I hear? Go quickly and chase the
seductor away.

BASILIO:
(What a time to have arrived!)
Pardon me, my lord.

SUSANNA: *(staggering)*
What a disaster! What wretchedness!
I'm overwhelmed by grief.

BASILIO ed IL CONTE:
Ah già svien la poverina!
Come, oh Dio, le batte il cor!

BASILIO:
Pian pianin su questo seggio.

SUSANNA:
Dove sono?
Cosa veggio!
Che insolenza, andate fuor!

BASILIO:
Siamo qui per aiutarvi,
e sicuro il vostro onor.

IL CONTE:
Siamo qui per aiutarti,
non turbarti, oh mio tesor.

BASILIO:
Ah, del paggio quel che ho detto
era solo un mio sospetto.

SUSANNA:
È un'insidia, una perfidia,
non credete all'impostor.

IL CONTE:
Parta, parta il damerino!

SUSANNA e BASILIO:
Poverino!

IL CONTE:
Poverino!
Ma da me sorpreso ancor.

SUSANNA e BASILIO:
Come! Che!

IL CONTE:
Da tua cugina l'uscio ier trovai rinchiuso;
picchio, m'apre Barbarina paurosa fuor
dell'uso.Io dal muso insospettito, guardo, cerco
in ogni sito, ed alzando pian pianino il tappetto al
tavolino vedo il paggio.

BASILIO and COUNT:
Ah, the poor creature is almost fainting!
Oh God, how her heart beats!

BASILIO: *(trying to seat Susanna)*
Easy, easy, sit down on this chair.

SUSANNA:
Where am I?
What do I see?
What impertinence! Go away!

BASILIO:
We're here to help you,
and secure your honor.

COUNT:
We're here to help you,
don't be disturbed, my treasure.

BASILIO: *(to the Count)*
What I said about the page was only my
suspicion.

SUSANNA:
And a scandalous lie!
Don't believe him. He's a faker.

COUNT:
Let the dandy depart!

SUSANNA and BASILIO:
The poor little one!

COUNT:
The poor little one!
But yet more surprises for me.

SUSANNA and BASILIO:
How? What?

COUNT:
The door was shut at your cousin's. I knocked,
and Barbarina opened the door, appearing
quite frightened. Because of her suspicion I
searched all over. Then I lifted the cloth from
the table, and I find the page hiding.

As the Count describes his experience, he lifts the gown that covers the chair,
and to his surprise, he discovers Cherubino.

Ah! cosa veggio?	Oh! What do I see?

SUSANNA:
(Ah! Crude stelle!)

SUSANNA:
(Oh! Cruel stars!)

BASILIO:
(Ah! Meglio ancora!)

BASILIO:
(Oh! How delightful!)

IL CONTE:
Onestissima signora!
Or capisco come va!

COUNT: *(to Susanna)*
Most virtuous lady!
Now I understand how things go!

SUSANNA:
(Accader non può di peggio,
giusti Dei! Che mai sarà!)

SUSANNA:
(Nothing worse could have happened!
Gods! What will happen?)

BASILIO:
Così fan tutte le belle; non c'è alcuna novità!

BASILIO:
All the beautiful women do the same;
there's nothing else new!

IL CONTE:
Basilio, in traccia tosto di Figaro volate:
io vo' ch'ei veda.

COUNT: *(pointing to Cherubino)*
Basilio. Hurry quickly and get Figaro. I want
him to see this for himself.

SUSANNA:
Ed io che senta; andate!

SUSANNA:
And I want him to hear, so get going!

IL CONTE:
Restate: che baldanza! E quale scusa
se la colpa è evidente?

COUNT: *(to Susanna)*
You stay! What assurance and what excuse can
you make if the guilt is evident?

SUSANNA:
Non ha d'uopo di scusa un'innocente.

SUSANNA:
Innocence needs no excuse.

IL CONTE:
Ma costui quando venne?

COUNT:
When did he come here to be with you?

SUSANNA:
Egli era meco quando voi qui giungeste, e mi
chiedea d'impegnar la padrona a intercedergli
grazia. Il vostro arrivo in scompiglio lo pose,
ed allor in quel loco si nascose.

SUSANNA:
He was with me when you arrived, and was
begging me to intercede with Madame for her
compassion. Your arrival scared him, and then
he decided to hide himself.

IL CONTE:
Ma s'io stesso m'assisi quando in camera entrai!

COUNT: *(to Cherubino)*
You were already in the room when I arrived?

CHERUBINO:
Ed allor di dietro io mi celai.

CHERUBINO:
And then I hid myself behind the chair.

IL CONTE:
E quando io là mi posi?

COUNT: (pointing)
And when I hid myself there?

CHERUBINO:
Allor io pian mi volsi, e qui m'ascosi.

CHERUBINO:
Then I quietly turned and hid myself.

IL CONTE:
Oh ciel, dunque ha sentito tutto quello ch'io ti dicea!

COUNT: (to Susanna)
Oh Heavens. Then you heard everything that I was saying!

CHERUBINO:
Feci per non sentir quanto potea.

CHERUBINO:
I made believe that I heard nothing.

IL CONTE:
Ah perfidia!

COUNT:
Treachery!

BASILIO:
Frenatevi: vien gente!

BASILIO:
Hurry, people are coming!

IL CONTE:
E voi restate qui, picciol serpente!

COUNT: (to Cherubino)
And you stay here, little serpent!

Peasants enter, followed by Figaro.

CORO:
Giovani liete, fiori spargete
davanti al nobile nostro signor.
Il suo gran core vi serba intatto
d'un più bel fiore l'almo candor.

CHORUS:
Happy youngsters, spread flowers before our noble lord.
His gracious heart and sincerity has preserved virtue.

IL CONTE:
Cos'è questa commedia?

COUNT: (to Figaro)
What is this show all about?

FIGARO:
(Eccoci in danza: secondami cor mio.)

FIGARO: (whispering to Susanna)
(We're beginning, play up to me, my love.)

SUSANNA:
(Non ci ho speranza.)

SUSANNA:
(There's no hope.)

FIGARO:
Signor, non sdegnate questo del nostro affetto
meritato tributo: or che aboliste
un diritto sì ingrato a chi ben ama.

FIGARO:
Sir, don't scorn our deserved and worthy tribute to you. You abolished a right that you held very dear.

IL CONTE:
Quel diritto or non v'è più; cosa si brama?

COUNT:
That privilege is abolished, so what else do you want?

FIGARO:
Della vostra saggezza il primo frutto
oggi noi coglierem: le nostre nozze
si son già stabilite. Or a voi tocca
costei che un vostro dono
illibata serbò, coprir di questa,
simbolo d'onestà, candida vesta.

IL CONTE:
(Diabolica astuzia! Ma fingere convien.)
Son grato, amici, ad un senso sì onesto!
Ma non merto per questo né tributi, né lodi; e
un dritto ingiusto ne' miei feudi abolendo, a
natura, al dover lor dritti io rendo.

TUTTI:
Evviva, evviva, evviva!

SUSANNA:
Che virtù!

FIGARO:
Che giustizia!

IL CONTE:
A voi prometto compier la ceremonia:
chiedo sol breve indugio; io voglio in faccia
de' miei più fidi, e con più ricca pompa
rendervi appien felici.
(Marcellina si trovi.)
Andate, amici.

CORO:
Giovani liete, fiori spargete
davanti al nobile nostro signor.
Il suo gran core vi serba intatto
d'un più bel fiore l'almo candor.

FIGARO, SUSANNA e BASILIO:
Evviva!

FIGARO:
I'm the first happy bridegroom to receive the
benefit of your decree. Susanna and I are to be
married this very day, so by your gift, I will
receive her as a virtuous bride, and it would
please me if you would place the symbol of
virtue upon her head.

COUNT:
(Clever plotting! I won't be deceived.)
Friends, I am grateful for your loyal devotion!
But it was only my duty to reform these abuses,
and I deserve no praise for having abolished
what offended both virtue and nature.

ALL:
Hail the lord!

SUSANNA:
Noble words!

FIGARO:
What justice!

COUNT: *(to Figaro and Susanna)*
I promise to perform the ceremony for you
later. It will be a public ceremony with all the
proper pomp and circumstance.
(aside)
(We must find Marcellina.)
Let's go, friends.

CHORUS:
Happy youngsters, spread flowers before our
noble lord.
His gracious heart and sincerity has preserved
virtue.

FIGARO, SUSANNA, BASILIO:
Hail!

The peasants depart.

FIGARO:
E voi non applaudite?

SUSANNA:
È afflitto poveretto! Perché il padron lo scaccia
dal castello!

FIGARO:
Ah, in un giorno sì bello!

FIGARO: *(to the sad Cherubino)*
And why don't you applaud?

SUSANNA:
He is grieved because the Count turned him
out of the castle.

FIGARO:
On such a happy day!

SUSANNA:
In un giorno di nozze!

FIGARO:
Quando ognun v'ammira!

CHERUBINO
Perdono, mio signor.

IL CONTE:
Nol meritate.

SUSANNA:
Egli è ancora fanciullo!

IL CONTE:
Men di quel che tu credi.

CHERUBINO:
È ver, mancai; ma dal mio labbro alfine...

IL CONTE:
Ben ben; io vi perdono. Anzi farò di più;
vacante è un posto d'uffizial nel reggimento
mio; io scelgo voi; partite tosto: addio.

SUSANNA:
On a wedding day!

FIGARO:
When every one admires you!

CHERUBINO: *(kneeling to the Count)*
Pardon me my lord.

COUNT:
You don't deserve it

SUSANNA:
He's just a mere child.

COUNT:
Not so young as you think.

CHERUBINO:
It is true I erred, but I will never mention...

COUNT:
Well, well. I pardon you. But I'll do even more
for you. There is an official post vacant in my
regiment. I appoint you there. Leave immediately.
Farewell.

The Count tries to leave but is stopped by Figaro and Susanna.

SUSANNA e FIGARO:
Ah, fin domani sol.

IL CONTE:
No, parta tosto.

CHERUBINO:
A ubbidirvi, signor, son già disposto.

IL CONTE:
Via, per l'ultima volta la Susanna abbracciate.
(Inaspettato è il colpo.)

SUSANNA and FIGARO:
But let him leave tomorrow.

COUNT:
No, he leaves right now.

CHERUBINO:
I am ready to obey you, my lord.

COUNT: *(ironically)*
Go. Susanna will embrace you for the last
time. (The blow indeed surprised them.)

The Count departs.

FIGARO:
Ehi, capitano, a me pure la mano;
io vo' parlarti pria che tu parta.
Addio, picciolo Cherubino; come cangia in un
punto il tuo destino.

FIGARO:
Hey, captain, let's shake hands.
I want to speak to you before you leave. Farewell,
little Cherubino, how quickly your destiny has
changed.

Vivace
FIGARO

Non più andrai, far - fallon - e a - mo - ro - so,

Non più andrai, farfallone amoroso,
notte e giorno d'intorno girando;
delle belle turbando il riposo
Narcisetto, Adoncino d'amor.

Non più avrai questi bei pennacchini,
quel cappello leggero e galante,
quella chioma, quell'aria brillante,
quel vermiglio donnesco color.

Tra guerrieri, poffar Bacco!
Gran mustacchi, stretto sacco.
Schioppo in spalla, sciabla al fianco,
collo dritto, muso franco, un gran casco, o un gran
turbante, molto onor, poco contante!

Ed invece del fandango,
una marcia per il fango.
Per montagne, per valloni,
con le nevi e i sollioni.

Al concerto di tromboni,
di bombarde, di cannoni,
che le palle in tutti i tuoni all'orecchio fan
fischiar. Cherubino alla vittoria:
alla gloria militar.

You'll no longer be fluttering around night and
day like an amorous butterfly troubling all the
sleeping beauties, little Narcissus, little loving
Adonis.

You'll no longer have those pretty feathers,
that light and gallant hat, that head of hair, that
sparkling air, and those rosy cheeks.

Among soldiers, by Jupiter, you'll have a large
mustache, bushy whiskers, and a short tunic:
on your shoulders a gun, a sword at your side,
and a big helmet and large turban. Much honor
but little money.

Instead of the fandango, a nice march through
mud, climbing mountains, crossing valleys,
now through the snow, and then in the heat.

You'll hear many sounds in your ears: bugles,
explosions, cannons, and shells hissing and
whizzing by.
Cherubino, rush to victory and a soldier's
glory.

ACT II

The Countess's sumptuous and opulent bedroom.

Larghetto
COUNTESS

Por - gi a - mor,   qualche ri - sto - ro,

LA CONTESSA: Porgi, amor, qualche ristoro al mio duolo, a' miei sospir. O mi rendi il mio tesoro, o mi lascia almen morir.	**COUNTESS:** Cupid, love, give me consolation, to my pain and sorrows. Restore my treasured love, or if not, at least leave me to die.

Susanna enters carrying a dress.

LA CONTESSA: Vieni, cara Susanna, finiscimi l'istoria!	**COUNTESS:** Come dear Susanna, finish the story!
SUSANNA: È già finita.	**SUSANNA:** It is already finished.
LA CONTESSA: Dunque volle sedurti?	**COUNTESS:** Then he wanted to seduce you?
SUSANNA: Oh, il signor Conte non fa tai complimenti colle donne mie pari; egli venne a contratto di danari.	**SUSANNA:** Oh, the Count doesn't give such compliments to women of my status; with us he offers money.
LA CONTESSA: Ah, il crudel più non m'ama!	**COUNTESS:** Oh, that cruel man no longer loves me!
SUSANNA: E come poi è geloso di voi?	**SUSANNA:** Then why is he so jealous of you?
LA CONTESSA: Come lo sono i moderni mariti: per sistema infedeli, per genio capricciosi, e per orgoglio poi tutti gelosi. Ma se Figaro t'ama, ei sol potria...	**COUNTESS:** All modern husbands are that way. They're unfaithful and fickle on principle, but their pride causes them to be jealous. But if Figaro loves you, you may be certain...
FIGARO: La la la....	**FIGARO:** *(enters singing)* La la la....

SUSANNA:
Eccolo: vieni, amico.
Madama impaziente.

FIGARO:
A voi non tocca stare in pena per questo.
Alfin di che si tratta?
Al signor Conte piace la sposa mia,
indi segretamente ricuperar vorria il diritto
feudale. Possibile è la cosa, e naturale.

LA CONTESSA:
Possibil?

SUSANNA
Naturale?

FIGARO:
Naturalissima. E se Susanna vuol
possibilissima.

SUSANNA:
Finiscila una volta.

FIGARO:
Ho già finito.
Quindi prese il partito di sceglier me corriero,
e la Susanna consigliera segreta d'ambasciata.
E perch'ella ostinata ognor rifiuta il diploma
d'onor ch'ei le destina minaccia di protegger
Marcellina.
Questo è tutto l'affare.

SUSANNA:
Ed hai coraggio di trattar scherzando
un negozio sì serio?

FIGARO:
Non vi basta che scherzando io ci pensi?

Ecco il progetto:
per Basilio un biglietto io gli fi capitar che
l'avvertisca di certo appuntamento che per
l'ora del ballo a un amante voi deste.

LA CONTESSA:
O ciel! Che sento!
Ad un uom sì geloso?

SUSANNA:
Here he is. *(and then to Figaro)*
Come, Madame is quite anxious.

FIGARO: *(to the Countess)*
Don't be so uneasy about this.
What are we really dealing with?
The Count secretly admires my intended wife,
and his possible reason is that he wants to
restore his feudal rights. That may be the
reason, and it's natural.

COUNTESS:
Possible?

SUSANNA:
Natural?

FIGARO:
Perfectly natural. And if Susanna is willing,
very possible.

SUSANNA:
Stop talking like that.

FIGARO:
I'm already finished.
That's why he decided to take me to London as
a courier, and Susanna as "confidential attaché"
to the embassy. And because she is persistently
obstinate and refuses the diplomatic honor, he's
created a menace for me and protects
Marcellina. That's the whole story.

SUSANNA:
And you have the audacity to treat such a
serious matter as a joke?

FIGARO:
Aren't you thankful that I do treat it lightly?

Here's my plan:
I'll use Basilio to take an anonymous letter to
the Count that advises him that the Countess
has made an appointment to meet her secret
lover at the ball.

COUNTESS:
Oh heavens! What am I hearing?
And to a man who is so jealous?

FIGARO:
Ancora meglio!
Così potrem più presto imbarazzarlo,
confonderlo, imbrogliarlo, rovesciargli i
progetti, empierlo di sospetti, e porgli in testa
che la moderna festa ch'ei di fare a me tenta
altri a lui faccia; onde qua perda il tempo, ivi
la traccia. Così quasi ex abrupto, e senza
ch'abbia fatto per frastonarci alcun disegno
vien l'ora delle nozze, e in faccia a lei non fia,
ch'osi d'opporsi ai voti miei.

SUSANNA:
È ver, ma in di lui vece s'opporrà Marcellina.

FIGARO:
Aspetta! Al Conte farai subito dir, che verso
sera attendati in giardino,
il picciol Cherubino per mio consiglio non
ancora partito da femmina vestito,
faremo che in sua vece ivi sen vada.
Questa è l'unica strada onde monsù sorpreso da
madama sia costretto a far poi quel che si brama.

LA CONTESSA:
Che ti par?

SUSANNA:
Non c'è mal.

LA CONTESSA:
Nel nostro caso....

SUSANNA:
Quand'egli è persuaso....e dove è il tempo?

FIGARO:
Il Conte è alla caccia; e per qualch'ora
non sarà di ritorno; io vado e tosto
Cherubino vi mando; lascio a voi
la cura di vestirlo.

LA CONTESSA:
E poi?

FIGARO:
E poi....
Se vuol ballare signor Contino, il chitarrino le
suonerò.

FIGARO:
So much the better!
Then we can embarrass him more quickly,
confound him, embroil him, overturn his
plans, fill him with suspicions, and put in his
mind that we can both play the same intrigues.
We'll make him waste the entire day searching
for the culprit, and suddenly, before he can
interfere with our plan, it will be time for us to
be married, and his opposition would be useless.

SUSANNA:
Perhaps, but you're not counting on
Marcellina opposing the wedding..

FIGARO:
Wait! Let the Count know that toward evening
the Countess will meet little Cherubino in the
garden, and that his departure was delayed on
my advisement. We'll dress him as a woman in
female clothes. This is the only way to get
Madame to catch the Count red-handed, and
then we can make him do what we want.

COUNTESS: *(to Susanna)*
What do you think?

SUSANNA:
Not too bad.

COUNTESS:
In our situation....

SUSANNA:
When he's persuaded....and when do we do it?

FIGARO:
The Count is hunting and it will be some time
before he returns. I'll go and get Cherubino,
and send him here so you can dress him.

COUNTESS:
And then?

FIGARO:
And then....
If you want to dance, my Count,
my guitar will accompany you.

Figaro exits

LA CONTESSA:
Quanto duolmi, Susanna, che questo giovin-otto abbia del Conte le stravaganze udite! Ah tu non sai! Ma per qual causa mai Da me stessa ei non venne? Dov'è la canzonetta?

COUNTESS:
Susanna, I'm not happy that this young boy has heard the Count's foolishness! Oh, why did he go to you and not come to me? Where is the little song he wrote?

SUSANNA:
Eccola: appunto facciam che ce la canti. Zitto, vien gente! È desso.

Avanti, avanti, signor uffiziale.

SUSANNA:
Here it is. Let's make him sing it. Quiet, someone's coming! It's him.
(Cherubino enters)
Come in, come in, gallant officer.

CHERUBINO:
Ah, non chiamarmi con nome sì fatale! Ei mi rammenta che abbandonar degg'io comare tanto buona.

CHERUBINO:
Oh, don't call me by that awful title! It reminds me that I must part from my kind and gentle godmother.

SUSANNA:
E tanto bella!

SUSANNA:
And so beautiful!

CHERUBINO:
Ah sì, certo!

CHERUBINO: *(sighing)*
Oh, yes, certainly!

SUSANNA:
Ah sì, certo! Ipocritone! Via presto la canzone che stamane a me deste a madama cantate.

SUSANNA: *(mimicking him)*
Oh, yes, certainly! Hypocrite! Quickly, sing the song to Madame that you gave me this morning.

LA CONTESSA:
Chi n'è l'autor?

COUNTESS:
Who wrote the song?

SUSANNA:
Guardate: egli ha due braccia di rossor sulla faccia.

SUSANNA: *(pointing to Cherubino)*
Look! His cheeks are red and he's blushing all over.

LA CONTESSA
Prendi la mia chitarra, e l'accompagna.

COUNTESS:
Take my guitar and accompany him.

CHERUBINO
Io sono sì tremante, ma se madama vuole.

CHERUBINO:
I'm trembling all over, but if Madame wishes.

SUSANNA
Lo vuole, sì, lo vuol. Manco parole.

SUSANNA:
She indeed wishes it, so keep your word.

Andante

Voi, che sa - pe - te che co - sa è amor,

CHERUBINO
Voi che sapete che cosa è amor,
donne, vedete s'io l'ho nel cor.
Quello ch'io provo vi ridirò,
è per me nuovo, capir nol so.
Sento un affetto pien di desir,
ch'ora è diletto, ch'ora è martir.
Gelo e poi sento l'alma avvampar,
e in un momento torno a gelar.
Ricerco un bene fuori di me,
non so chi'l tiene, non so cos'è.

Sospiro e gemo senza voler,
palpito e tremo senza saper.
Non trovo pace notte né dì,
Eppur mi piace languir così.

CHERUBINO:
You indeed know what love is.
Look ladies, if I have it in my heart.
I'll tell you what I feel.
It's all new to me. I don't understand it.
I feel a passion that is full of desire,
at times I feel torment, at times delight.
And then I feel frozen, then on fire.
and in an instant, frozen again.
I seek happiness from another,
I don't know who has it, or what it is.

I sigh and suffer without knowing.
I throb and tremble without knowing why.
I find no peace night or day,
Yet I am pleased to languish this way.

LA CONTESSA:
Bravo! Che bella voce! Io non sapea
che cantaste sì bene.

COUNTESS:
Great! What a beautiful voice! I didn't know
he could sing so well.

SUSANNA:
Oh, in verità egli fa tutto ben quello ch'ei fa.
Presto a noi, bel soldato;
Figaro v'informò....

SUSANNA:
Oh, Indeed, everything he does he does well.
Come here, gallant soldier.
Figaro told you....

CHERUBINO:
Tutto mi disse.

CHERUBINO:
He told me everything.

SUSANNA:
Lasciatemi veder. Andrà benissimo!
Siam d'uguale statura.Giù quel manto.

SUSANNA: *(measuring Cherubino)*
Let me see. It will be fine!
We're the same height. Take off your coat.

LA CONTESSA:
Che fai?

COUNTESS:
What are you doing?

SUSANNA:
Niente paura.

SUSANNA:
Don't be afraid.

LA CONTESSA:
E se qualcuno entrasse?

COUNTESS:
And what if someone comes?

SUSANNA:
Entri, che mal facciamo?
La porta chiuderò.
Ma come poi acconciargli i cappelli?

SUSANNA:
Let them, what are we doing wrong?
I'll close the door. *(locks the door)*
But how should we arrange his hair?

LA CONTESSA:
Una mia cuffia prendi nel gabinetto.
Presto!

COUNTESS:
Take one of my bonnets from the cabinet.
Hurry!

While Susanna goes to a cabinet to get a bonnet,
Cherubino approaches the Countess and shows her his commission.

Che carta è quella?	What is this paper?

CHERUBINO:
La patente.

CHERUBINO:
The commission.

LA CONTESSA:
Che sollecita gente!

COUNTESS:
What urgency!

CHERUBINO:
L'ebbi or da Basilio.

CHERUBINO:
I just received it from Basilio.

The Countess notices a ribbon tied on Cherubino's arm.

LA CONTESSA
Dalla fretta obliato hanno il sigillo.

COUNTESS:
In their haste they forgot the seal.

SUSANNA:
Il sigillo di che?

SUSANNA:
What seal?

LA CONTESSA:
Della patente.

COUNTESS:
For the commission.

SUSANNA:
Cospetto! Che premura!
Ecco la cuffia.

SUSANNA:
Indeed! What haste!
Here is the bonnet.

LA CONTESSA:
Spicciati: va bene!
Miserabili noi, se il Conte viene.

COUNTESS:
Do be quick! It seems to be fine!
We're in trouble if the Count should come.

Allegretto
SUSANNA

Ve - nite   in- gi - noc - chia-tevi,

SUSANNA:
Venite, inginocchiatevi, restate fermo lì.

SUSANNA: *(dressing Cherubino)*
Come, kneel down, and stay still.

Pian piano, or via, giratevi:
bravo, va ben così.

Very gently turn around.
Great! That's good.
(Cherubino looks toward the Countess)

La faccia ora volgetemi!
Olà, quegli occhi a me!

Turn your face to me!
Hey, yours eyes to me!

Drittissimo: guardatemi.
Madama qui non è.

Look right into my face.
Madame is not here.

Restate fermo, or via,
giratevi, bravo!
Più alto quel colletto,
quel ciglio un po' più basso,
le mani sotto il petto,
vedremo poscia il passo,
quando sarete in piè.

Stay still here, or go,
turn to me, great!
Your neck higher,
and cast down those wicked eyes,
hands under your chest,
when you stand up
we'll see how you walk.

Mirate il bricconcello!
Mirate quanto è bello!
Che furba guardatura!
Che vezzo, che figura!
Se l'amano le femmine
han certo il lor perché.

Look at the rascal!
Look how handsome he is!
What cunning glances he has!
What charm, what a figure!
If women love him,
they certainly have good reason.

LA CONTESSA:
Quante buffonerie!

COUNTESS:
What clowning!

SUSANNA:
Ma se ne sono io medesma gelosa; ehi,
serpentello, volete tralasciar d'esser sì bello?

SUSANNA:
I'm afraid I'm going to be jealous myself. You
little devil, how dare you be so handsome?

LA CONTESSA:
Finiam le ragazzate; or quelle maniche
oltre il gomito gli alza, onde più agiatamente
l'abito gli si adatti.

COUNTESS:
Let's stop being ridiculous.
Tuck up those sleeves above the elbow so that
the dress won't agitate him so much.

SUSANNA:
Ecco.

SUSANNA:
There.

LA CONTESSA:
Più indietro.
Così.

COUNTESS:
Farther back.
Like so.

The Countess reads the commission and notices that the seal is missing.

Che nastro è quello?

What is that ribbon?

SUSANNA:
È quel ch'esso involommi.

SUSANNA:
He stole it from me.

LA CONTESSA:
E questo sangue?

COUNTESS:
And it's bloodstained?

CHERUBINO:
Quel sangue io non so come, poco pria
sdrucciolando in un sasso la pelle io mi
graffiai e la piaga col nastro io mi fasciai.

CHERUBINO:
I don't know how that blood got there.
A little earlier I slipped on a rock. The stone cut
me and I tied the cut with the ribbon.

SUSANNA:
Mostrate! Non è mal; cospetto! Ha il braccio più
candido del mio! Qualche ragazza.

SUSANNA:
Show me! It's not bad! His arm is whiter than
mine, white like a lady's arm.

LA CONTESSA:
E segui a far la pazza?
Va nel mio gabinettto, e prendi un poco
d'inglese taffetà, ch'è sullo scrigno.

In quanto al nastro, inver, per il colore
mi spiacea di privarmene.

SUSANNA:
Tenete, e da legargli il braccio?

LA CONTESSA:
Un altro nastro prendi insieme col mio vestito.

CHERUBINO:
Ah, più presto m'avria quello guarito!

LA CONTESSA:
Perché? Questo è migliore!

CHERUBINO:
Allor che un nastro legò la chioma ovver toccò
la pelle d'oggetto...

LA CONTESSA:
Forastiero, è buon per le ferite, non è vero?
Guardate qualità ch'io non sapea!

CHERUBINO:
Madama scherza, ed io frattanto parto.

LA CONTESSA:
Poverin! Che sventura!

CHERUBINO:
Oh, me infelice?

LA CONTESSA:
Or piange.

CHERUBINO:
Oh ciel! Perché morir non lice!
Forse vicino all'ultimo momento
questa bocca oseria!

LA CONTESSA:
Siete saggio, cos'è questa follia!

Chi picchia alla mia porta?

COUNTESS:
Why do I follow this craziness?
Go to my cabinets and get a bit of English
adhesive plaster that's on the jewel box.
(Susanna leaves quickly)
About that ribbon, I'll keep it. It's a color that
suits me.

SUSANNA: *(returning)*
Should I tie it on his arm?

COUNTESS:
Take another piece of ribbon from my dress.

CHERUBINO:
DO it quickly so I can heal!

COUNTESS:
Why? This is better!

CHERUBINO:
I have a feeling that if a ribbon has touched
the hair of someone...

COUNTESS:
If it's from a stranger it's good for the wound.
Right? I've never realized it was of such quality!

CHERUBINO:
Madame mocks me, and I must leave.

COUNTESS:
Poor one! How unfortunate!

CHERUBINO:
Oh, how can I bear it?

COUNTESS:
Then cry.

CHERUBINO:
Oh heavens! I'd like to die now!
Perhaps at the last moment, I might kiss that
mouth!

COUNTESS:
What nonsense you are speaking!

(a knocking at the door)
Who knocks at the door?

IL CONTE:
Perché è chiusa?

COUNT: *(from outside)*
Why is the door closed?

LA CONTESSA:
Il mio sposo! Oh Dei! Son morta!
Voi qui, senza mantello! In quello stato,
un ricevuto foglio, la sua gran gelosia!

COUNTESS:
My husband! Oh Gods! I'm finished!
You here, and undressed! In that condition, a
letter received, his great jealousy!

IL CONTE:
Cosa indugiate?

COUNT:
Why do you delay?

LA CONTESSA:
Son sola, ah sì, son sola.

COUNTESS:
I'm alone, yes, alone.

IL CONTE:
E a chi parlate?

COUNT:
Then who were you speaking with?

LA CONTESSA:
A voi, certo, a voi stesso.

COUNTESS:
To you...certainly to you alone.

CHERUBINO:
Dopo quel ch'è successo, il suo furore,
non trovo altro consiglio!

CHERUBINO:
After what has happened, and his anger,
there's only one thing to do!

Cherubino runs to the closet and closes the door behind him.

LA CONTESSA:
Ah, mi difenda il cielo in tal periglio!

COUNTESS: *(take the key)*
Oh heaven help me in such danger!

The Countess unlocks the door and admits the Count.

IL CONTE:
Che novità! Non fu mai vostra usanza
di rinchiudervi in stanza.

COUNT:
What's the idea! You never used to lock
yourself in your room!

LA CONTESSA:
È ver; ma io, io stava qui mettendo.

COUNTESS:
True, but I, I was trying.

IL CONTE:
Via, mettendo...

COUNT:
You were trying...

LA CONTESSA:
Certe robe; era meco la Susanna,
che in sua camera è andata.

COUNTESS:
Certain clothes. Susanna was here with me but
has gone to her room.

IL CONTE:
Ad ogni modo voi non siete tranquilla.

Guardate questo foglio.

COUNT:
In any sense you're not relaxed.
(The Count shows her a letter)
Look at this paper.

LA CONTESSA:
(Numi! È il foglio che Figaro gli scrisse!)

COUNTESS: *(aside)*
(Gods! It's the letter Figaro wrote to him!)

A noise is heard from the closet where Cherubino hides.

IL CONTE:
Cos'è codesto strepito?
In gabinetto qualche cosa è caduta.

COUNT:
What is that noise?
Something fell down in the closet.

LA CONTESSA:
Io non intesi niente.

COUNTESS:
I didn't hear anything.

IL CONTE:
Convien che abbiate i gran pensieri in mente.

COUNT:
It is clear that you must have many things on
your mind.

LA CONTESSA:
Di che?

COUNTESS:
About what?

IL CONTE
Là v'è qualchuno.

COUNT: *(becoming suspicious)*
Somebody is in there.

LA CONTESSA:
Chi volete che sia?

COUNTESS:
Who do you think it is?

IL CONTE:
Lo chiedo a voi; io vengo in questo punto.

COUNT:
I ask you. I just arrived here.

LA CONTESSA:
Ah sì, Susanna, appunto.

COUNTESS:
Oh, yes, it's Susanna, of course.

IL CONTE:
Che passò, mi diceste, alla sua stanza!

COUNT:
You just told me Susanna went to her room!

LA CONTESSA:
Alla sua stanza, o qui, non vidi bene.

COUNTESS:
To her room, or here. I didn't see well.

IL CONTE:
Susanna, e donde viene che siete sì turbata?

COUNT:
Susanna, so why are you so disturbed now?

LA CONTESSA:
Per la mia cameriera?

COUNTESS:
For my maid?

IL CONTE:
Io non so nulla; ma turbata senz'altro.

COUNT:
I know nothing, but undoubtedly you're upset.

LA CONTESSA:
Ah, questa serva più che non turba me turba
voi stesso.

COUNTESS:
Oh, that maid upsets me more than ever, and
she disturbs you also.

IL CONTE:
È vero, è vero, e lo vedrete adesso.

COUNT:
It's true, and you'll see now.

(The Count goes toward the closet)

IL CONTE:
Susanna, or via, sortite, sortite, io così vo'.

COUNT:
Susanna, come out now, come out. I order you.

LA CONTESSA:
Fermatevi! Sentite!
Sortire ella non può.

COUNTESS:
Stay there! Hear me!
Susanna cannot come out.

SUSANNA:
(Cos'è codesta lite?
Il paggio dove andò?)

SUSANNA:
(What does this mean?
Where did the page go?)

(The Count searches the alcove)

IL CONTE:
E chi vietarlo or osa?

COUNT:
And who can forbid or dare me now?

LA CONTESSA:
Lo vieta l'onestà. Un abito da sposa
provando ella si sta.

COUNTESS:
Modesty prevents it. She's trying on her
wedding dress.

IL CONTE:
(Chiarissima è la cosa: l'amante qui sarà.)

COUNT:
(It is clear to me that her lover is in there.)

LA CONTESSA:
(Bruttissima è la cosa, chi sa cosa sarà.)

COUNTESS:
(This is horrible. How will it end?)

SUSANNA:
(Capisco qualche cosa, veggiamo come va.)

SUSANNA:
(I understand only a little. Let's see how this
will work out.)

IL CONTE:
Dunque parlate almeno. Susanna, se qui siete.

COUNT:
Susanna, if you're in the room, at least speak.

LA CONTESSA:
Nemmen, nemmen, nemmeno,
io v'ordino: tacete.

COUNTESS:
Never, never, never, I command you to be
quiet.

(Susanna hides herself in the alcove.)

IL CONTE:
Consorte mia, giudizio, un scandalo, un
disordine, schiviam per carità!

COUNT:
Be prudent, my wife, and let's avoid a scandal
or a messy quarrel!

SUSANNA:
Oh cielo, un precipizio, un scandalo, un
disordine, qui certo nascerà.

SUSANNA:
At this point, a scandal or messy quarrel, will
certainly erupt.

LA CONTESSA
Consorte mio, giudizio, un scandalo, un
disordine, schiviam per carità!

IL CONTE:
Dunque voi non aprite?

LA CONTESSA:
E perché degg'io le mie camere aprir?

IL CONTE:
Ebben, lasciate, l'aprirem senza chiavi. Ehi?
Gente?

LA CONTESSA:
Come? Porreste a repentaglio d'una dama
l'onore?

IL CONTE:
È vero, io sbaglio. Posso senza rumore,
senza scandalo alcun di nostra gente
andar io stesso a prender l'occorrente.
Attendete pur qui, ma perché in tutto
sia il mio dubbio distrutto anco le porte
io prima chiuderò.

LA CONTESSA:
(Che imprudenza!)

IL CONTE:
Voi la condiscendenza di venir meco avrete.
Madama, eccovi il braccio, andiamo.

LA CONTESSA:
Andiamo.

IL CONTE:
Susanna starà qui finché torniamo.

COUNTESS:
Be prudent, my husband, and let's avoid a messy
quarrel!

COUNT:
Then you're not opening the door?

COUNTESS:
And why must I open my rooms?

COUNT:
Then, leave me. I'll open them without keys.
Who's in there? A person?

COUNTESS: *(restraining him)*
What? Would you jeopardize the honor of a
woman of rank?

COUNT:
It's true. I'm wrong. I can do it without scandal
in front of the servants. I'll go myself and fetch
the tools to do it.
It would be better if you wait here to avoid any
intrigue. I'm going to lock every door in the
room.

COUNTESS: *(aside)*
(What impudence!)

COUNT:
You will have the discretion to come with me
Madame. Here is my arm. Let's go.

COUNTESS:
Let' go.

COUNT:
Susanna will be here until we return.

After the Count and Countess leave,
Susanna rushes from the alvoce to the closet door.

SUSANNA:
Aprite, presto, aprite; aprite, è la Susanna.
Sortite, via sortite, andate via di qua.

CHERUBINO:
Oimè, che scena orribile!
Che gran fatalità!

SUSANNA: *(to Cherubino)*
Open, open quickly. Open, it's Susanna.
Come out, come out, get away from here.

CHERUBINO:
Oh my, what a horrible predicament!
What an awful fate!

SUSANNA:
Partite, non tardate di qua, di là.

SUSANNA e CHERUBINO:
Le porte son serrate, che mai, che mai sarà?

CHERUBINO:
Qui perdersi non giova.

SUSANNA:
V'uccide se vi trova.

CHERUBINO:
Veggiamo un po' qui fuori. Dà proprio nel
giardino.

SUSANNA:
Fermate, Cherubino!
Fermate per pietà!

SUSANNA:
Tropp'alto per un salto, fermate per pietà!

CHERUBINO:
Lasciami, pria di nuocerle nel fuoco volerei.
Abbraccio te per lei.
addio, così si fa.

SUSANNA:
Leave. Don't delay. This way, that way.

SUSANNA and CHERUBINO:
The doors are locked. What shall we do?

CHERUBINO:
I'm finished if I stay here.

SUSANNA:
He'll kill you if he finds you here.

CHERUBINO: *(looks out the window)*
Then I'll use the window. It looks right into the
garden. *(Cherubino prepares to jump)*

SUSANNA:
Stop! Cherubino!
Stop for heaven's sake!

SUSANNA:
Stop, it's too high for you to jump.

CHERUBINO:
Leave me alone. I would fly into the fire before
hurting her. I embrace you for her.
(kisses Susanna) Farewell, this is the way to do it.

Cherubino jumps from the window as Susanna looks after him.

SUSANNA:
Oh, guarda il demonietto! Come fugge!
È già un miglio lontano.
Ma non perdiamoci invano.
Entriam nel gabinetto.
venga poi lo smargiasso, io qui l'aspetto.

SUSANNA:
Oh, look at the little devil! How he flees!
He's already a mile away.
But we haven't lost each other in vain.
I'll enter the closet, wait for them,
and let the fury come.

Susanna enters the closet and closes the door behind her.
The Count and Countess return. The Count holds an iron bar
to break open the closet door. He searches the room suspiciously.

IL CONTE:
Tutto è come il lasciai; volete dunque
aprir voi stessa, o deggio.

COUNT:
Every thing is as when I left. Will you then open
the door yourself, or must I.

LA CONTESSA:
Ahimé, fermate; e ascoltatemi un poco.
Mi credete capace di mancar al dover?

COUNTESS:
Stop and listen to me. Do you think that I am
capable of being unfaithful?

IL CONTE:
Come vi piace. Entro quel gabinetto
chi v'è chiuso vedrò.

COUNT:
As you please. I intend to see who is hiding in
that closet.

LA CONTESSA:
Sì, lo vedrete, ma uditemi tranquillo.

COUNTESS:
Yes, you shall, but hear me calmly.

IL CONTE:
Non è dunque Susanna?

COUNT:
Then it is not Susanna?

LA CONTESSA:
No, ma invece è un oggetto,
che ragion di sospetto
non vi deve lasciar: per questa sera
una burla innocente di far si disponeva, ed io
vi giuro che l'onor, l'onestà.

COUNTESS:
No, someone else is in there, one whose
intentions are harmless, and whom you have no
right to suspect. I was preparing some harmless
entertainment for this evening's amusement,
and I swear I have done nothing wrong.

IL CONTE:
Chi è dunque! Dite, l'ucciderò.

COUNT:
Who is it? Tell me and I'll kill him.

LA CONTESSA:
Sentite!
(Ah, non ho cor!)

COUNTESS:
Listen!
(I can't speak!)

IL CONTE:
Parlate.

COUNT:
Speak.

LA CONTESSA:
È un fanciullo.

COUNTESS:
He is a mere child.

IL CONTE:
Un fanciul!

COUNT:
A child!

LA CONTESSA:
Sì, Cherubino.

COUNTESS:
Yes, Cherubino.

IL CONTE:
(E mi farà il destino ritrovar questo paggio in
ogni loco!)
Come? Non è partito? Scellerati!
Ecco i dubbi spiegati, ecco l'imbroglio,
ecco il raggiro, onde m'avverte il foglio.

COUNT:
(Why do my unlucky stars make me find this
page everywhere?)
What? He hasn't left? Scoundrels!
Now my suspicions are verified, and now I
understand that anonymous letter.

Raging, the Count goes towards the closet.

Allegro
COUNT

E - sci o mai, garzon mal - na -to, scia - gu - ra - to, non tardar!

IL CONTE:
Esci omai, garzon malnato,
sciagurato, non tardar.

COUNT:
Come out now, uncouth lad, scoundrel, and
don't delay.

LA CONTESSA:
Ah! Signore, quel furore, per lui fammi il cor
tremar.

COUNTESS:
Sir, your rage makes me tremble for him!

IL CONTE:
E d'opporvi ancor osate?

COUNT:
Why do you still dare to interfere?

LA CONTESSA:
No, sentite.

COUNTESS:
No, listen.

IL CONTE:
Via parlate.

COUNT:
Then tell me.

LA CONTESSA:
Giuro al ciel ch'ogni sospetto,
e lo stato in che il trovate.
Sciolto il collo! Nudo il petto!

COUNTESS:
I swear by Heaven that he is innocent, even
though you'll find him in shirt sleeves and
bear chested!

IL CONTE:
Sciolto il collo!
Nudo il petto! Seguitate!

COUNT:
In his shirt sleeves!
Bear chested! Let's go then!

LA CONTESSA:
Per vestir femminee spoglie.

COUNTESS:
It was all to dress him as a lady.

IL CONTE:
Ah! Comprendo, indegna moglie,
mi vo' tosto vendicar.

COUNT:
Yes, I now understand, unfaithful wife.
I will take revenge immediately.

(takes the crow in a rage.)

LA CONTESSA:
Mi fa torto quel trasporto, m'oltraggiate a
dubitar.

COUNTESS:
Your passion wrongs me, and you offend me
by your doubts.

IL CONTE:
Qua la chiave!

COUNT:
Give me the key!

LA CONTESSA:
Egli è innocente. Voi sapete.

COUNTESS: *(hands him the key)*
He is innocent. You know.

IL CONTE:
Non so niente! Va lontan dagl'occhi miei!
Un'infida, un'empia sei, e mi cerchi
d'infamar.

COUNT:
I know nothing. Go far from my sight. You are
a faithless and false woman, and you seek to
dishonor me.

The Count enters the closet.

LA CONTESSA:
Vado, sì, ma....

COUNTESS:
I'll go, but....

IL CONTE:
Non ascolto.

COUNT:
I will not listen to you.

LA CONTESSA:
Non son rea.

COUNTESS:
I am guiltless.

IL CONTE:
Vel leggo in volto!
Mora, mora, e più non sia, ria cagion del mio penar.

COUNT:
I read it in your face!
Let him die, and no longer be the cause of all my sufferings.

LA CONTESSA:
Ah! La cieca gelosia qualche eccesso gli fa far.

COUNTESS:
His blind, excessive jealousy will provoke a catastrophe.

The Count draws his sword, and opens the door. The Countess, overwhelmed by fear, covers her eyes. Susanna stands at the doorway with a grave and ironical air.

IL CONTE:
Susanna!

COUNT:
Susanna!

LA CONTESSA:
Susanna!

COUNTESS:
Susanna!

SUSANNA:
Signore! Cos'è quel stupore?
Il brando prendete, il paggio uccidete!
Quel paggio malnato, vedetelo qua.

SUSANNA:
Sir! Why such astonishment?
You take up your sword to kill the page, and you see the traitor before you.

IL CONTE:
(Che scola! La testa girando mi va.)

COUNT:
(What can this mean? I'm baffled and confused.)

LA CONTESSA:
(Che storia è mai questa, Susanna v'è là.)

COUNTESS:
(What is this, Susanna there.)

SUSANNA:
(Confusa han la testa, non san come va.)

SUSANNA:
(Their heads are confused, and they don't know what is going on.)

IL CONTE:
Sei sola?

COUNT:
Are you alone?

SUSANNA:
Guardate, qui ascoso sarà.

SUSANNA:
Look inside and find what you can.

IL CONTE:
Guardiamo, qui ascoso sarà.

COUNT:
Let's look, and find what we can.

LA CONTESSA:
Susanna, son morta, il fiato mi manca.

COUNTESS:
Susanna, I tremble and I am faint.

SUSANNA:
Più lieta, più franca, in salvo è di già.

SUSANNA: *(pointing to the window)*
Be more cheerful, the boy is safe.

The Count emerges from the closet.

IL CONTE:
Che sbaglio mai presi! Appena lo credo; se a torto v'offesi perdono vi chiedo; ma far burla simile è poi crudeltà.

COUNT: *(addresses the Countess)*
What a mistake I made! I can hardly believe it! If I have wronged you. I beg your forgiveness, But such foolish jokes indeed are too cruel.

LA CONTESSA e SUSANNA:
Le vostre follie non mertan pietà.

COUNTESS and SUSANNA::
Your follies deserve no mercy at all.

IL CONTE:
Io v'amo.

COUNT:
I love you.

LA CONTESSA:
Nol dite!

COUNTESS:
You're not truthful!

IL CONTE:
Vel giuro.

COUNT:
I swear it.

COUNTESS:
Mentite. Son l'empia, l'infida che ognora v'inganna.

COUNTESS:
Deceiver! I am an honorable woman who has never deceived you.

IL CONTE:
Quell'ira, Susanna, m'aita a calmar.

COUNT:
Susanna, help me to appease her anger!

SUSANNA:
Così si condanna chi può sospettar.

SUSANNA:
One capable of such suspicion, must be punished accordingly.

LA CONTESSA:
Adunque la fede d'un'anima amante sì fiera mercede doveva sperar?

COUNTESS:
What has been my reward for years of faithful devotion?

SUSANNA:
Signora!

SUSANNA:
Madam!

IL CONTE:
Rosina!

COUNT:
Rosina!

LA CONTESSA:
Crudele! Più quella non sono; ma il misero oggetto del vostro abbandono che avete diletto di far disperar.

COUNTESS:
Cruel husband! I will no longer be the unfortunate object of your contempt, your delight that drives me to despair.

IL CONTE:
Confuso, pentito, son troppo punito,
abbiate pietà.

COUNT:
I am confused and penitent. Have mercy, it is
too much punishment.

SUSANNA:
Confuso, pentito, è troppo punito,
abbiate pietà.

SUSANNA:
I am confused and penitent. Have mercy, it is
too much punishment.

LA CONTESSA:
Soffrir sì gran torto quest'alma non sa.

COUNTESS:
My soul can not bear such great insults.

IL CONTE:
Ma il paggio rinchiuso?

COUNT:
The page wasn't there?

LA CONTESSA:
Fu sol per provarvi.

COUNTESS:
It was only to test you.

IL CONTE:
Ma i tremiti, i palpiti?

COUNT:
But your trembling and anxiety?

LA CONTESSA:
Fu sol per burlarvi.

COUNTESS:
It was to just to make some fun.

(the Count shows the letter.)

IL CONTE:
Ma un foglio sì barbaro?

COUNT:
But what did this cruel letter mean?

LA CONTESSA e SUSANNA:
Di Figaro è il foglio, e a voi per Basilio.

COUNTESS and SUSANNA:
The writer was Figaro, and Basilio the bearer.

IL CONTE:
Ah perfidi! Lo voglio.

COUNT:
I'll punish the scoundrels.

LA CONTESSA e SUSANNA:
Perdono non merta chi agli altri nol da.

COUNTESS and SUSANNA:
He is undeserving of pardon, something he
will not grant to others.

IL CONTE:
Ebben, se vi piace comune è la pace;
Rosina inflessibile con me non sarà.

COUNT:
Well then, if you like, we'll make peace.
Rosina will not be uncompromising with me.

LA CONTESSA:
Ah quanto, Susanna, son dolce di core!
Di donne al furore chi più crederà?

COUNTESS:
Oh Susanna, how gentle my heart is!
Who can believe women's anger?

In a gesture of reconciliation, the Countess offers her band to the Count.

SUSANNA:
Cogl'uomin, signora, girate, volgete,
vedrete che ognora si cade poi là.

SUSANNA:
Madame, these men who turn and wiggle all
the same.

IL CONTE:
Guardatemi!

COUNT:
Look at me!

LA CONTESSA:
Ingrato!

COUNTESS:
Ungrateful man!

IL CONTE:
Ho torto, e mi pento.

COUNT:
I erred, and I repent.

IL CONTE, LA CONTESSA, SUSANNA:
Da questo momento quest'alma a conoscermi/
conoscerla/conoscervi
apprender potrà.

COUNT, COUNTESS, SUSANNA: This soul
will now learn to know (her/me/ you) quite
well.

Figaro arrives.

FIGARO:
Signori, di fuori son già i suonatori.
Le trombe sentite, i pifferi udite, tra canti, tra
balli de' nostri vassalli
corriamo, voliamo le nozze a compir.

FIGARO::
The musicians have already arrived.
Hear the trumpets and the pipers, and the
dancing and singing. Let's hurry and
celebrate the wedding.

As Figaro begins to leave, the Count stops him.

IL CONTE:
Pian piano, men fretta.

COUNT:
Gently, gently, not so fast.

FIGARO:
La turba m'aspetta.

FIGARO:
The people expect me.

IL CONTE:
Un dubbio toglietemi in pria di partir.

COUNT:
Before you go, rid me of a doubt.

LA CONTESSA, SUSANNA ,FIGARO:
(La cosa è scabrosa; com'ha da finir!)

COUNTESS, SUSANNA, FIGARO:
(It is a rough point; how is it to end?)

IL CONTE:
(Con arte le carte convien qui scoprir.)

COUNT:
(I must play my cards skilfully.)

The Count shows Figaro the letter.

Conoscete, signor Figaro, questo foglio chi
vergò?

Do you know, Mr. Figaro, who wrote this
letter?

FIGARO:
Nol conosco.

FIGARO:
I do not.

LA CONTESSA, IL CONTE, SUSANNA:
Nol conosci?

COUNTESS, COUNT, SUSANNA:
You do not?

FIGARO:
No, no, no!

FIGARO:
I don't know.

SUSANNA:
E nol desti a Don Basilio.

LA CONTESSA:
Per recarlo....

IL CONTE:
Tu c'intendi.

FIGARO:
Oibò, oibò.

SUSANNA:
E non sai del damerino

LA CONTESSA:
Che stasera nel giardino...

IL CONTE:
Già capisci?

FIGARO:
Io non lo so.

IL CONTE:
Cerchi invan difesa e scusa, il tuo ceffo già
t'accusa, vedo ben che vuoi mentir.

FIGARO:
Mente il ceffo, io già non mento.

LA CONTESSA e SUSANNA
Il talento aguzzi invano palesato abbiam
l'arcano, non v'è nulla da ridir.

IL CONTE:
Che rispondi?

FIGARO:
Niente, niente.

IL CONTE:
Dunque accordi?

FIGARO:
Non accordo.

LA CONTESSA e SUSANNA:
Eh via, chetati, balordo, la burletta ha da finir.

SUSANNA:
Didn't you give it to Don Basilio?

COUNTESS:
To deliver....

COUNT:
You don't understand.

FIGARO:
Not I, no, no.

SUSANNA:
And about the rendezvous.

COUNTESS:
For this evening in the garden...

COUNT:
Do you know now?

FIGARO::
I know nothing.

COUNT:
Your defence and excuses are hopeless.
Your face accuses you, and I see that you lie.

FIGARO:
My face lies, but not I.

COUNTESS and SUSANNA::
It is in vain for you to sharpen your wit; we
have discovered the secret; there is nothing to
repeat.

COUNT:
What do you answer?

FIGARO:
Nothing, nothing.

COUNT:
Then you agree?

FIGARO:
I do not agree.

COUNTESS and SUSANNA:
Come, mad fellow, you must finish the farce.

FIGARO:
Per finirla lietamente e all'usanza teatrale
un'azion matrimoniale le faremo ora seguir.

LA CONTESSA, SUSANNA, FIGARO:
Deh signor, nol contrastate, consolate i lor/
miei desir.

IL CONTE:
(Marcellina, Marcellina!
Quanto tardi a comparir!)

FIGARO:
To finish it joyfully according to theatrical
custom, we shall have a wedding entertainment
to follow now.

COUNTESS, SUSANNA, FIGARO:
Pray, sir, do not oppose it. Grant the wishes
and console me/them.

COUNT:
(Marcellina, Marcellina!
How long you have delayed!)

The gardener Antonio enters, half drunk, and carrying a broken flower pot.

ANTONIO:
Ah! Signor! Signor!.

IL CONTE:
Cosa è stato?

ANTONIO:
Che insolenza! Chi'l fece? Chi fu?

**IL COUNT, LA CONTESSA,
SUSANNA,FIGARO:**
Cosa dici, cos'hai, cosa è nato?

ANTONIO:
Ascoltate!

**LA CONTESSA, COUNT, SUSANNA, e
FIGARO:**
Via, parla, di', su.

ANTONIO:
Dal balcone che guarda in giardino
mille cose ogni dì gittar veggio,
e poc'anzi, può darsi di peggio,
vidi un uom, signor mio, gittar giù.

IL CONTE:
Dal balcone?

ANTONIO:
Vedete i garofani!

IL CONTE:
In giardino?

ANTONIO:
Oh! My lord! My lord!

COUNT:
What is the matter?

ANTONIO:
What impudence! What happened? Who was it?

**COUNT, COUNTESS, SUSANNA,
FIGARO:**
What is this all about? What happened?

ANTONIO:
Listen to me!

**COUNTESS, COUNT, FIGARO and
SUSANNA:**
Come, speak out.

ANTONIO: *(to the Count.)*
Every day they throw down rubbish from the
balcony into the garden. But a little while ago,
it was worse: I saw a man throw himself out.

COUNT:
From the balcony?

ANTONIO: *(showing the vase)*
See the pink carnations!.

COUNT:
In the garden?

SUSANNA, LA CONTESSA:

(Figaro, all'erta.)

IL CONTE:
Cosa sento?

SUSANNA, LA CONTESSA, FIGARO:
Costui ci sconcerta, quel briaco che viene far qui?

IL CONTE:
Dunque un uom! Ma dov'è, dov'è gito?

ANTONIO:
Ratto, ratto, il birbone è fuggito, e ad un tratto di vista m'uscì.

SUSANNA:
Sai che il paggio.

FIGARO:
So tutto, lo vidi.
Ah, ah, ah!

IL CONTE:
Taci là.

ANTONIO:
Cosa ridi?

FIGARO:
Tu sei cotto dal sorger del dì.

IL CONTE:
Or ripetimi, un uom dal balcone.

ANTONIO:
Dal balcone.

IL CONTE:
In giardino.

ANTONIO:
In giardino.

SUSANNA, LA CONTESSA , FIGARO:
Ma, signore, se in lui parla il vino!

SUSANNA, COUNTESS:
(whispering to Figaro)
(Now, Figaro, you must be sharp.)

COUNT:
What do I hear?

SUSANNA, COUNTESS, FIGARO:
This is disconcerting. Who let this drunk in here?

COUNT: (to Antonio)
Then a man! But where has he gone?

ANTONIO:
The scoundrel ran away full speed, and I immediately lost sight of him.

SUSANNA: (whispering to Figaro)
You know that it was the page.

FIGARO: (whispering to Susanna)
I know all, I saw him.
Ha, ha, ha!

COUNT:
Be quiet over there.

ANTONIO: (to Figaro)
Why do you laugh?

FIGARO:
Because you're drunk all day.

COUNT: (to Antonio)
Now repeat it, a man from the balcony.

ANTONIO:
From the balcony.

COUNT:
In the garden.

ANTONIO:
In the garden.

SUSANNA, COUNTESS, FIGARO:
But, sir, it is the wine that speaks in him!

IL CONTE:
Segui pure, né in volto il vedesti?

ANTONIO:
No, nol vidi.

SUSANNA, LA CONTESSA:
(Olá, Figaro, ascolta!)

FIGARO:
Via, piangione, sta zitto una volta,
per tre soldi far tanto tumulto!

Giacché il fatto non può star occulto,
sono io stesso saltato di lì.

IL CONTE:
Chi? Voi stesso?

SUSANNA, LA CONTESSA:
Che testa! Che ingegno!

FIGARO:
Che stupor!

ANTONIO:
Chi? Voi stesso?

IL CONTE:
Già creder nol posso.

ANTONIO:
Come mai diventaste sì grosso?
Dopo il salto non foste così.

FIGARO:
A chi salta succede così.

ANTONIO:
Chi'l direbbe.

SUSANNA e LA CONTESSA:
Ed insiste quel pazzo!

IL CONTE:
Tu che dici?

ANTONIO:
A me parve il ragazzo.

IL CONTE:
Cherubin!

COUNT: *(to Antonio)*
Go on. Did you see his face?

ANTONIO:
No I did not.

SUSANNA, COUNTESS:
(Listen Figaro, and be sharp!)

FIGARO: *(to Antonio, pointing to the flowers)*
Come, crying booby, hold your tongue.
To make such a noise for threepence!

Since it can no longer hide it, I was the one
who jumped down from there.

COUNT:
Who? It was you?

SUSANNA, COUNTESS:
(What a head! How clever!)

FIGARO: *(to the Count)*
Why wonder?

ANTONIO: *(to Figaro)*
Who? It was you?

COUNT:
I can not believe it.

ANTONIO: *(to Figaro)*
You've grown quite a bit since your fall?
I would swear you were just half the size.

FIGARO:
It happens that was to people who jump.

ANTONIO:
Who would have thought it?

SUSANNA, COUNTESS:
And that idiot still insists!

COUNT: *(to Antonio)*
What did you say?

ANTONIO:
I thought it was the boy.

COUNT:
Cherubino!

SUSANNA, LA CONTESSA:
Maledetto!

FIGARO:
Esso appunto da Siviglia a cavallo qui giunto,
da Siviglia ov'ei forse sarà.

ANTONIO:
Questo no, questo no, che il cavallo
io non vidi saltare di là.

IL CONTE:
Che pazienza! Finiam questo ballo!

SUSANNA, LA CONTESSA:
(Come mai, giusto ciel, finirà?)

IL CONTE:
Dunque tu?.

FIGARO:
Saltai giù.

IL CONTE:
Ma perché?

FIGARO:
Il timor.

IL CONTE:
Che timor?

FIGARO:
Là rinchiuso aspettando quel caro visetto,
tippe tappe, un sussurro fuor d'uso.
voi gridaste, lo scritto biglietto,
saltai giù dal terrore confuso,
e stravolto m'ho un nervo del pie'!

ANTONIO:
Vostre dunque saran queste carte
che perdeste.

IL CONTE:
Olà, porgile a me.

FIGARO:
Sono in trappola.

SUSANNA e LA CONTESSA:
(Figaro, all'erta.)

SUSANNA, COUNTESS:
Curse him!

FIGARO:
Of course. He just returned today from Seville
on horseback.

ANTONIO:
Not so, not so, for I didn't see the horse jump
down.

COUNT:
What patience! Let us finish this inquiry!

SUSANNA, COUNTESS:
(Good heavens! How will it end?)

COUNT: *(to Figaro)*
So it was you?

FIGARO:
I jumped down.

COUNT:
Why then?

FIGARO:
Fear.

COUNT:
What fear?

FIGARO:
I was waiting in there for Susanna, when I
heard a babel of voices. Your voice was angry,
and I thought about this letter. So I jumped
from this window in terror, and twisted my
foot in the fall.

ANTONIO:
Then these papers are that were dropped are
yours.

COUNT:
Here! Give them to me.

FIGARO: *(to the Countess and Susanna)*
I am caught in a trap.

SUSANNA, COUNTESS:
(Figaro, be on the alert!

IL CONTE:
Dite un po', questo foglio cos'è?

COUNT:
Tell me a little what the paper is about?
(showing it him at a distance.)

FIGARO:
Tosto, tosto, n' ho tanti, aspettate!

FIGARO:
Just a moment, and I'll tell you.

Figaro takes many papers out of his pocket and examines them.

ANTONIO:
Sarà forse il sommario de' debiti.

ANTONIO:
Perhaps it is a list of his debts.

FIGARO:
No, la lista degl'osti.

FIGARO:
No, a list of your wine shops.

IL CONTE:
Parlate.
E tu lascialo; e parti.

COUNT: *(to Figaro)*
Speak!
(to Antonio) And you can leave now.

SUSANNA, LA CONTESSA e FIGARO:
Lascialo.(Lasciami) e parti.

SUSANNA, COUNTESS, FIGARO:
Leave him (me) and go.

ANTONIO:
Parto, sì, ma se torno a trovarti.

ANTONIO:
I'll go, yes, but if I find you again

FIGARO:
Vanne, vanne, non temo di te.

FIGARO:
Go, go, I do not fear you.

Antonio exits. The Count displays the paper to everyone.

IL CONTE:
Dunque.

COUNT:
Well then.

LA CONTESSA:
(O ciel! La patente del paggio!)

COUNTESS: *(aside to Susanna)*
(Oh heavens! The page's commission!)

SUSANNA:
Giusti Dei, la patente!

SUSANNA: *(aside to Figaro)*
Oh heavens, the commission!)

IL CONTE:
Coraggio!

COUNT: *(to Figaro)*
Cheer up.

FIGARO:
O che testa! Questa è la patente che poc'anzi il fanciullo mi diè.

FIGARO:
Oh what a head! That is the commission which the boy gave me a while ago.

IL CONTE:
Per che fare?

COUNT:
What for?

FIGARO:
Vi manca....

FIGARO:
It needed....

IL CONTE:
Vi manca?

COUNT:
It needed?

LA CONTESSA
(Il suggello.)

COUNTESS: *(aside to Susanna)*
(The seal.)

SUSANNA:
(Il suggello.)

SUSANNA: *(aside to Figaro)*
(The seal.)

IL CONTE:
Rispondi.

COUNT:
Answer.

FIGARO:
È l'usanza...

FIGARO:
Well, it's usual...

IL CONTE:
Su via, ti confondi?

COUNT:
Come on, answer me quickly?

FIGARO:
È l'usanza di porvi il suggello.

FIGARO:
It is usual to seal a commission.

IL CONTE:
(Questo birbo mi toglie il cervello,
tutto, tutto è un mistero per me.)

COUNT: *(tearing up the paper)*
(This rascal is too much for my patience.
All of this is a mystery to me.)

SUSANNA e LA CONTESSA:
(Se mi salvo da questa tempesta
più non avvi naufragio per me.)

SUSANNA, COUNTESS:
(If I save myself from this storm, I shall never
fear a shipwreck!)

FIGARO:
(Sbuffa invano e la terra calpesta;
poverino ne sa men di me.)

FIGARO:
(You can bluster and rage all you want, but I
know more than you do.)

Marcellina, Bartolo and Basilio enter excitedly.

MARCELLINA, BASILIO, BARTOLO:
Voi signor, che giusto siete ci dovete ascoltar.

MARCELLINA, BASILIO, BARTOLO:
Just lord, you must hear us now.

IL CONTE:
(Son venuti a vendicarmi io mi sento a
consolar.)

COUNT:
(They've come to avenge me, and I feel myself
comforted!)

SUSANNA, LA CONTESSA, FIGARO:
(Son venuti a sconcertarmi qual rimedio
ritrovar?)

SUSANNA, COUNTESS, FIGARO:
They are come to put me out; what remedy can
I find!

FIGARO:
Son tre stolidi, tre pazzi, cosa mai vengono a
far?

FIGARO: *(to the Count)*
These three stupid, mad ones, what have they
come here for?

IL CONTE:
Pian pianin, senza schiamazzi dica ognun quel che gli par.

MARCELLINA:
Un impegno nuziale ha costui con me contratto, e pretendo che il contratto deva meco effettuar.

SUSANNA, LA CONTESSA, FIGARO:
Come! Come!

IL CONTE:
Olà, silenzio! Io son qui per giudicar.

BARTOLO:
Io da lei scelto avvocato vengo a far le sue difese, le legittime pretese, io qui vengo a palesar.

SUSANNA, LA CONTESSA, FIGARO:
È un birbante!

IL CONTE:
Olà, silenzio! Io son qui per giudicar.

BASILIO:
Io, com'uom al mondo cognito vengo qui per testimonio del promesso matrimonio con prestanza di danar.

SUSANNA, LA CONTESSA, FIGARO:
Son tre matti.

IL CONTE:
Olà, silenzio! Lo vedremo, il contratto leggeremo, tutto in ordin deve andar.

SUSANNA, LA CONTESSA e FIGARO:
Son confusa/o, son stordita/o, disperata/o, sbalordita/o. Certo un diavol dell'inferno qui li ha fatti capitar.

MARCELLINA, BASILIO, BARTOLO, IL CONTE:
Che bel colpo! Che bel caso!
È cresciuto a tutti il naso, qualche nume a noi propizio qui ci/li ha fatti capitar.

COUNT:
Softly and gently, and without confusion, let everyone speak his peace.

MARCELLINA: *(pointing to Figaro)*
This man signed a marriage contract with me, and I appeal to you to make him fulfill his contract.

SUSANNA, COUNTESS, FIGARO:
What's this! What's this!

COUNT:
Be silent, I'm the judge here.

BARTOLO:
I appear for this lady as her counsel in this action, demanding performance of the contract, and damages in full.

SUSANNA, COUNTESS, FIGARO:
He's a scoundrel!

COUNT:
Be silent, I'm the judge here.

BASILIO:
I bear witness that the plaintiff lent him money on the condition that if he could not repay her, he agreed to marry her.

SUSANNA, COUNTESS, FIGARO:
The three of them are crazy.

COUNT:
No more! The contract shall be read, and I myself will discover the truth.

SUSANNA, COUNTESS, FIGARO:
I am confused, I am astonished, in despair and confounded! Certainly the infernal devil has sent them here.

MARCELLINA, BARTOLO, BASILIO, COUNT:
What a fine blow! What a fine case! It has raised our esteem! It was Providence that brought us all here.

ACT III

A large hall in the Count's palace. The Count paces to and fro,
reflecting his skepticism and suspicion about recent events.

IL CONTE:
Che imbarazzo è mai questo!
Un foglio anonimo. la cameriera in gabinetto
chiusa, la padrona confusa un uom che salta
dal balcone in giardino, un altro appresso che
dice esser quel desso.

Non so cosa pensar? Potrebbe forse qualcun
de' miei vassalli? A simil razza
è comune l'ardir, ma la Contessa.
Ah, che un dubbio l'offende. Ella rispetta
troppo sé stessa, e l'onor mio, l'onore.
Dove diamin l'ha posto umano errore!

COUNT:
What a perplexing situation!
An anonymous letter, the maid locked in the
closet, my lady embarrassed, a man jumps
from the balcony into the garden, and another
who says that he was the one.

What could it all mean? Could it have been
one of my vassals? There's no limit to what
they will dare. But the Countess. No I won't
insult her. She has too high a sense of her
dignity, and mine as well! I must admit that
human nature is frail.

The Countess looks in, and then brings in Susanna.

LA CONTESSA:
Via, fatti core: digli
che ti attenda in giardino.

COUNTESS: *(aside to Susanna)*
Come, take courage, tell him to wait for you in
the garden.

The Countess withdraws, leaving the Count and Susanna alone.

IL CONTE
Saprò se Cherubino era giunto a Siviglia. A
tale oggetto ho mandato Basilio.

COUNT: *(still in deep thought)*
I shall know if Cherubino had arrived at
Seville. For that purpose I sent Basilio.

SUSANNA:
Oh cielo! E Figaro?

SUSANNA: *(to the Countess)*
:O gods! And Figaro?

LA CONTESSA:
A lui non dei dir nulla: in vece tua
voglio andarci io medesma.

COUNTESS:
Don't say a word to him! I'll keep the
appointment myself.

IL CONTE:
Avanti sera dovrebbe ritornar.

COUNT:
Basilio will return before evening.

SUSANNA:
Oh Dio! Non oso.

SUSANNA:
Oh God! I don't dare.

LA CONTESSA:
Pensa, ch'è in tua mano il mio riposo.

COUNTESS:
Remember, all my happiness depends on it.

IL CONTE:
E Susanna? Chi sa ch'ella tradito
abbia il segreto mio, oh, se ha parlato,
gli fo sposar la vecchia.

COUNT:
And Susanna? Who knows whether she has
betrayed my secret. If she has spoken, I'll make
the old woman marry Figaro.

SUSANNA:
(Marcellina!) Signor!.

IL CONTE:
Cosa bramate?

SUSANNA:
Mi par che siete in collera!

IL CONTE:
Volete qualche cosa?

SUSANNA:
Signor, la vostra sposa ha i soliti vapori,
e vi chiede il fiaschetto degli odori.

IL CONTE:
Prendete.

SUSANNA:
Or vel riporto.

IL CONTE:
Ah no, potete ritenerlo per voi.

SUSANNA:
Per me? Questi non son mali da donne triviali.

IL CONTE:
Un'amante, che perde il caro sposo
sul punto d'ottenerlo.

SUSANNA:
Pagando Marcellina colla dote che voi mi
prometteste.

IL CONTE:
Ch'io vi promisi, quando?

SUSANNA:
Credea d'averlo inteso.

IL CONTE:
Sì, se voluto aveste intendermi voi stessa.

SUSANNA:
È mio dovere, e quel di Sua Eccellenza il mio
volere.

SUSANNA: *(coming forward)*
(Marcellina) Sir!

COUNT:
What do you want?

SUSANNA:
You seem to be angry!

COUNT:
Do you want something?

SUSANNA:
Your lady sent me because she's suffering from
the vapors, and wants tomorrow your.

COUNT:
Take it.

SUSANNA:
I'll bring it back soon.

COUNT:
Oh! no, you can keep it for yourself.

SUSANNA:
For me? Women in my position don't have
those ailments.

COUNT:
Not even a lover who loses her bridegroom just
before the wedding?

SUSANNA:
We'll pay Marcellina with the dowry that you
promised me.

COUNT:
That I promised you? When?

SUSANNA:
I thought I understood it that way.

COUNT:
Yes, if you would agree to my intentions.

SUSANNA:
It is my duty, and your lordship's pleasure is
my wish.

Andante
COUNT

Cru - del! Perchè fi - no - ra far - mi languir co - sì?

IL CONTE:
Crudel! Perché finora farmi languir così?

COUNT:
Cruel one! Why did you make me languish like this until now?

SUSANNA:
Signor, la donna ognora empo ha dir di sì.

SUSANNA:
My lord, a woman always has time to say yes.

IL CONTE:
Dunque, in giardin verrai?

COUNT:
Then you will come to the garden?

SUSANNA:
Se piace a voi, verrò.

SUSANNA:
If it pleases you, I will come.

IL CONTE:
E non mi mancherai?

COUNT:
And you will not disappoint me?

SUSANNA:
No, non vi mancherò.

SUSANNA:
No, I will not disappoint you.

IL CONTE:
Mi sento dal contento pieno di gioia il cor.

COUNT:
I feel my heart delighted, and filled with joy.

SUSANNA
Scusatemi se mento, voi che intendete amor.

SUSANNA:
If I do not deceive him, he'll only try again.

IL CONTE
E perché fosti meco stamattina sì austera?

COUNT:
Tell me why you treated me so severely this morning?

SUSANNA:
Col paggio ch'ivi c'era?

SUSANNA:
With the page listening?

IL CONTE:
Ed a Basilio che per me ti parlò?

COUNT:
And Basilio, who spoke to you for me?

SUSANNA:
Ma qual bisogno abbiam noi, che un Basilio?

SUSANNA:
What need do we have for a man like Basilio?

IL CONTE:
È vero, è vero, e mi prometti poi
se tu manchi, oh cor mio.
Ma la Contessa attenderà il fiaschetto.

COUNT:
You're right, my dear one, but promise me you won't disappoint me.
But my lady waits for the bottle.

SUSANNA:
Eh, fu un pretesto. Parlato io non avrei senza di questo.

SUSANNA:
Oh, that was only a pretext for me to be able to speak with you.

IL CONTE:
Carissima!

COUNT: *(taking Susanna's hand)*
My dearest!

SUSANNA:
Vien gente.

SUSANNA:
Someone's coming.

IL CONTE:
(È mia senz'altro.)

COUNT: *(aside)*
(Now I'm sure she's mine.)

SUSANNA:
(Forbitevi la bocca, oh signor scaltro.)

SUSANNA: *(aside)*
(You think that you're more cunning than me.)

Figaro enters.

FIGARO:
Ehi, Susanna, ove vai?

FIGARO:
Hey, Susanna, where are you?

SUSANNA:
Taci, senza avvocato hai già vinta la causa.

SUSANNA:
Quiet. You've won your case without an attorney.

FIGARO:
Cos'è nato?

FIGARO:
What has happened?

Susanna and Figaro depart.

IL CONTE:
Hai già vinta la causa! Cosa sento!
In qual laccio io cadea? Perfidi!

Io voglio di tal modo punirvi, a piacer mio la sentenza sarà.
Ma s'ei pagasse la vecchia pretendente?
Pagarla! In qual maniera!
E poi v'è Antonio, che a un incognito Figaro ricusa di dare una nipote in matrimonio.

Coltivando l'orgoglio di questo mentecatto, tutto giova a un raggiro, il colpo è fatto.

Vedrò mentre io sospiro, felice un servo mio!
E un ben ch'invan desio, ei posseder dovrà?
Vedrò per man d'amore unita a un vile oggetto chi in me destò un affetto che per me poi non ha?

COUNT: *(after overhearing them)*
You have already won your case! What do I hear? What trap did I fall into? Traitors!

I will punish you unmercifully with a sentence that pleases me.
But what if he paid off the old pretender?
He paid her! In what way!
Besides there's Antonio who will refuse to give his niece in marriage to the unknown Figaro.

Cultivating the pride of this dolt, all is in my favor, and the blow is struck by my trickery.

I will behold my happy servant while I sigh?
And are my passions in vain. Is he to possess my treasure? Shall I see joined by love an unworthy object who has raised my passion but feels nothing for me?

Ah no, lasciarti in pace, non vo' questo contento,
tu non nascesti, audace, per dare a me tormento,
e forse ancor per ridere di mia infelicità.
Già la speranza sola delle vendette mie
quest'anima consola, e giubilar mi fa.

Oh no! I will not be content to leave you in
peace. You audacious man. You were not born to
give me torment, and afterwards, laugh at my
misfortune.
Already the mere hope of my revenge consoles
my soul and fills me with joy.

Enter Figaro, Marcellina, Don Curzio, and Bartolo.

DON CURZIO:
È decisa la lite. O pagarla, o sposarla, ora
ammutite.

DON CURZIO: *(stuttering)*
It has been decided that he must pay her or
marry her.

MARCELLINA:
Io respiro.

MARCELLINA:
Now I'm happy.

FIGARO:
Ed io moro.

FIGARO:
And I am wretched.

MARCELLINA:
(Alfin sposa io sarò d'un uom ch'adoro.)

MARCELLINA:
(At last I'll marry the one I adore.)

FIGARO:
Eccellenza m'appello.

FIGARO:
My lord, I appeal.

IL CONTE:
È giusta la sentenza; o pagar, o sposar, bravo
Don Curzio.

COUNT:
The sentence is just; pay or marry.
Well done, Don Curzio.

DON CURZIO:
Bontà di sua Eccellenza.

DON CURZIO:
Your Excellency is kind.

BARTOLO:
Che superba sentenza!

BARTOLO:
What superb judgment!

FIGARO:
In che superba?

FIGARO:
In what way superb?

BARTOLO:
Siam tutti vendicati.

BARTOLO:
We are all avenged.

FIGARO:
Io non la sposerò.

FIGARO:
I won't marry her.

BARTOLO:
La sposerai.

BARTOLO:
You will marry her.

DON CURZIO:
O pagarla, o sposarla. Lei t'ha prestati
due mille pezzi duri.

DON CURZIO:
Pay her or marry her. She loaned you two
thousand crowns.

FIGARO:
Son gentiluomo, e senza l'assenso de' miei
nobili parenti.

FIGARO:
I am a gentleman, and without the consent of my
noble relatives

IL CONTE:
Dove sono? Chi sono?

COUNT:
Where am I? Who am I?

FIGARO:
Lasciate ancor cercarli; dopo dieci anni io
spero di trovarli.

FIGARO:
I wish someone would find them. I've spent
ten years searching for them.

BARTOLO:
Qualche bambin trovato?

BARTOLO:
You were found on the doorstep?

FIGARO:
No, perduto, dottor, anzi rubato.

FIGARO:
Not lost, Doctor, rather stolen.

IL CONTE:
Come?

COUNT:
How?

MARCELLINA:
Cosa?

MARCELLINA:
What?

BARTOLO:
La prova?

BARTOLO:
Where's proof?

DON CURZIO:
Il testimonio?

DON CURZIO:
Witnesses?

FIGARO
L'oro, le gemme, e i ricamati panni, che ne' più
teneri anni mi ritrovaro addosso i masnadieri,
sono gl'indizi veri di mia nascita illustre, e sopra
tutto questo al mio braccio impresso geroglifico.

FIGARO:
The gold, jewels, embroidered clothes, which
in my infancy the robbers found upon me, are
the true signs of my noble birth, and
particularly this hieroglyph printed on my arm.

Figaro turns up his sleeve and show the mark to everyone.

MARCELLINA:
Una spatola impressa al braccio destro?

MARCELLINA:
A spatula printed on your right arm?

FIGARO:
E a voi chi'l disse?

FIGARO:
Who told you about it?

MARCELLINA:
Oh Dio, è egli.

MARCELLINA:
Oh God, it is him.

FIGARO:
È ver son io.

FIGARO:
It is true what I am.

DON CURZIO, IL CONTE, BARTOLO:
Chi?

DON CURZIO, COUNT, BARTOLO:
Who?

MARCELLINA:
Raffaello!

BARTOLO:
E i ladri ti rapir.

FIGARO:
Presso un castello.

BARTOLO:
Ecco tua madre.

FIGARO:
Balia.

BARTOLO:
No, tua madre.

IL CONTE e DON CURZIO:
Sua madre!

FIGARO:
Cosa sento!

MARCELLINA:
Ecco tuo padre!

Riconosci in questo amplesso
una madre, amato figlio!

FIGARO:
Padre mio, fate lo stesso, non mi fate più
arrossir.

BARTOLO:
Resistenza la coscienza far non lascia al tuo desir.

DON CURZIO:
Ei suo padre, ella sua madre, l'imeneo non può
seguir.

IL CONTE:
Son smarrito, son stordito, meglio è assai di
qua partir.

MARCELLINA e BARTOLO:
Figlio amato!

FIGARO:
Parenti amati!

MARCELLINA:
Raffaello!

BARTOLO:
And stolen by robbers.

FIGARO:
Near a castle.

BARTOLO: *(pointing to Marcellina)*
Behold your mother.

FIGARO:
Nurse.

BARTOLO:
No, your mother.

COUNT and DON CURZIO::
His mother!

FIGARO:
What do I hear!

MARCELLINA: *(pointing to Bartolo)*
Here is your father.

(Marcellina embraces Figaro)
With this embrace, beloved son, recognize
your mother!

FIGARO: *(to Bartolo)*
My father, do the same. Don't make me blush
any longer.

BARTOLO: *(embracing Figaro)*
Conscience does not let me oppose your wish.

DON CURZIO: *(to the Count)*
He is the father, and she the mother.
The contract must be voided.

COUNT:
I am surprised, I am astonished. It would be
much better for me to leave here.

MARCELLINA and BARTOLO:
Beloved son!

FIGARO:
Beloved parents!

As the Count tries to depart, Susanna enters with a purse of money and stops him.

SUSANNA:
Alto,alto, signor Conte,
mille doppie son qui pronte,
a pagar vengo per Figaro,
ed a porlo in libertà.

SUSANNA:
Stop, stop, my lord, a thousand pistols are at the
ready here.
I have come to pay for Figaro,
and to restore his liberty.

IL CONTE e DON CURZIO:
Non sappiam com'è la cosa, osservate un poco
là!

COUNT, DON CURZIO:
We do not know your business, but look at
them over there!.

They point to Figaro who is embracing Marcellina.

SUSANNA:
Già d'accordo ei colla sposa; giusti Dei, che
infedeltà!

SUSANNA:
Already agreed with that bride! Just Gods,
what infidelity!

Susanna is about to leave, but Figaro stops her.

Lascia iniquo!

Leave me, villain!

FIGARO:
No, t'arresta! Senti, oh cara!

FIGARO:
No, stay and hear me, my love!

SUSANNA:
Senti questa!

SUSANNA: *(boxes his ears)*
Hear this one!

MARCELLINA, BARTOLO, FIGARO:
È un effetto di buon core, tutto amore è quel
che fa.

MARCELLINA, BARTOLO, FIGARO:
Here's resounding of a good heart, and proof
of passion.

IL CONTE:
Fremo, smanio dal furore, il destino a me la fa.

COUNT:
I fret, I rave with fury because fate is playing a
trick on me.

DON CURZIO:
Freme e smania dal furore, il destino gliela fa.

DON CURZIO:
He frets, he raves with fury because fate is
playing a trick on him.

SUSANNA:
Fremo, smanio dal furore, una vecchia a me la
fa.

SUSANNA:
I fret, I rave with fury because fate is playing a
trick on me.

MARCELLINA:
Lo sdegno calmate, mia cara figliuola,
sua madre abbracciate che or vostra sarà.

MARCELLINA: *(to Susanna)*
Calm your anger, my dear daughter. His mother
embraces you and will also be yours.

SUSANNA:
Sua madre?

SUSANNA:
His mother?

**BARTOLO, IL CONTE, DON CURZIO,
MARCELLINA:**
Sua madre!

**BARTOLO, COUNT, DON CURZIO,
MARCELLINA:**
His mother!

SUSANNA:
Tua madre?

SUSANNA: *(to Figaro)*
Your mother?

FIGARO:
E quello è mio padre che a te lo dirà.

FIGARO: *(pointing to Bartolo)*
This man will tell you he is my father.

SUSANNA:
Suo padre?

SUSANNA:
You father?

BARTOLO, IL CONTE, DON CURZIO,
MARCELLINA:
Suo padre!

BARTOLO, COUNT, DON CURZIO,
MARCELLINA:
His father!

SUSANNA:
Tuo padre?

SUSANNA: *(to Figaro)*
Your father?

FIGARO:
E quella è mia madre che a te lo dirà.

FIGARO:
And this one told you she is my mother.

All proceed to embrace each other.

SUSANNA, MARCELLINA, BARTOLO,
FIGARO
Al dolce contento di questo momento,
quest'anima appena resister or sa.

SUSANNA, MARCELLINA, BARTOLO,
FIGARO:
The soul can hardly sustain the sweet
contentment of this moment.

IL CONTE, DON CURZIO:
Al fiero tormento di questo momento,
quell'/quest'anima appena resister or sa.

COUNT, DON CURZIO:
My/his soul can hardly sustain the cruel
torment of this fatal moment.

The Count and Don Curzio depart.

MARCELLINA:
Eccovi, oh caro amico, il dolce frutto
dell'antico amor nostro.

MARCELLINA: *(to Bartolo)*
Take this, dear friend, the sweet fruits of our
old love.

BARTOLO
Or non parliamo di fatti sì rimoti, egli è mio
figlio, mia consorte voi siete; e le nozze farem
quando volete.

BARTOLO:
Let's not talk about old episodes. He is my
son, and you are my consort. We'll marry
whenever you want.

MARCELLINA:
Oggi, e doppie saranno.

Prendi, questo è il biglietto del danar che a me
devi, ed è tua dote.

MARCELLINA:
Today, a double wedding
(She gives the contract papers to Figaro)
Take this wedding present. It is the contract for
the money you owe me.

SUSANNA:
Prendi ancor questa borsa.

SUSANNA:
Take this purse too.

BARTOLO:
E questa ancora.

FIGARO:
Bravi, gittate pur ch'io piglio ognora.

SUSANNA:
Voliamo ad informar d'ogni avventura
madama e nostro zio.
Chi al par di me contenta!

FIGARO, BARTOLO, MARCELLINA:
Io!

TUTTI:
E schiatti il signor Conte al gusto mio.

BARTOLO:
And this one also.

FIGARO:
Well done! I'll take whatever you throw me.

SUSANNA: *(to Figaro)*
Let's rush to inform Madame and our uncle of
all that has happened.
Who can be as happy as I?

FIGARO, BARTOLO, MARCELLINA:
I am!

ALL:
And enlighten the Count of my happiness!

All leave happily.

Barbarina is pulling Cherubino by the hand.

BARBARINA:
Andiam, andiam, bel paggio, in casa mia
tutte ritroverai le più belle ragazze del castello,
di tutte sarai tu certo il più bello.

CHERUBINO:
Ah, se il Conte mi trova, misero me, tu sai che
partito ei mi crede per Siviglia.

BARBARINA:
O ve' che maraviglia, e se ti trova
non sarà cosa nuova.
Odi! Vogliamo vestirti come noi:
tutte insiem andrem poi
a presentar de' fiori a madamina;
fidati, oh Cherubin, di Barbarina.

BARBARINA:
Come, my handsome page. In my house you'll
find all the prettiest girls of the castle, but
you'll be the most beautiful.

CHERUBINO:
Oh, if the Count finds me, I am finished! You
know he thinks I've gone to Seville.

BARBARINA:
How marvelous. If he finds you it won't be the
first time.
Listen! We want to dress you like one of us,
and then we'll go to present some flowers to
my lady. Cherubino, trust Barbarina.

(Both exit.)

LA CONTESSA:
E Susanna non vien! Sono ansiosa
di saper come il Conte accolse la proposta.
Alquanto ardito il progetto mi par, e ad uno
sposo sì vivace, e geloso!

COUNTESS: *(alone)*
And Susanna hasn't come yet! I am anxious to
know how the Count received the proposal. The
plan seems to me a bold one for a husband so
quick and jealous.

Ma che mal c'è? Cangiando i miei vestiti
con quelli di Susanna, e i suoi co' miei
al favor della notte.
Oh cielo, a quale umil stato fatale io son
ridotta da un consorte crudel, che dopo avermi
con un misto inaudito d'infedeltà, di gelosia,
di sdegni, prima amata, indi offesa, e alfin
tradita, fammi or cercar da una mia serva aita!

But what harm is it in exchanging my clothes
with Susanna, and she wearing my evening
dress?
Oh Heavens! My cruel husband has humiliated
me with an unheard-of mixture of infidelity,
jealousy, and anger. First love, then offense,
and finally betrayal. And I am now compelled
to employ the assistance of my servant!

Andantino
COUNTESS

Do - ve so - no   i bei mo - men - ti

Dove sono i bei momenti di dolcezza e di
piacer, dove andaro i giuramenti
di quel labbro menzogner?Perché mai se in
pianti e in pene per me tutto si cangiò, la
memoria di quel bene
dal mio sen non trapassò?

Where are those charming moments of
sweetness and peace? Where have those
promises gone from those deceitful lips?
Why has my poor heart changed to sorrow
and pain from the beautiful memories I recall?

Ah! Se almen la mia costanza nel languire
amando ognor, mi portasse una speranza
di cangiar l'ingrato cor.

If only my constancy in loving, and my
suffering and pain could at least afford me a
hope to change that ungrateful heart.

The Countess exits.

The Count and Antonio enter. Antonio holds Cherubino's regimental hat.

ANTONIO:
Io vi dico, signor, che Cherubino è ancora nel
castello, e vedete per prova il suo cappello.

ANTONIO:.
I tell you, sir, that Cherubino is still in the
castle, and, as proof, here is his hat.

IL CONTE:
Ma come, se a quest'ora esser giunto a Siviglia
egli dovria.

COUNT:
How can he still be here when by this time he
ought to have arrived at Seville?

ANTONIO:
Scusate, oggi Siviglia è a casa mia, là vestissi
da donna, e là lasciati ha gl'altri abiti suoi.

ANTONIO:
Pardon me, but today Seville is in my house.
He's dressed as a female and has left his own
clothes in my house.

IL CONTE:
Perfidi!

COUNT:
Deceivers!

ANTONIO:
Andiam, e li vedrete voi.

ANTONIO:
Let us go, and you'll see them yourself.

After the Count and Antonio exit, the Countess and Susanna appear.

LA CONTESSA:
Cosa mi narri, e che ne disse il Conte?

COUNTESS:
And what did the Count say about it?

SUSANNA:
Gli si leggeva in fronte il dispetto e la rabbia.

SUSANNA:
One could read on his face that he was vexed
and enraged.

LA CONTESSA:
Piano, che meglio or lo porremo in gabbia.
Dov'è l'appuntamento che tu gli proponesti?

COUNTESS:
Gently, it'll be easier now to catch him.
Where did you propose to meet him?

SUSANNA:
In giardino.

SUSANNA:
In the garden.

LA CONTESSA:
Fissiamgli un loco. Scrivi.

COUNTESS:
Let's fix a spot. Write

SUSANNA:
Ch'io scriva, ma signora.

SUSANNA:
I write, but madam

LA CONTESSA:
Eh, scrivi dico; e tutto io prendo su me stessa:
"Canzonetta sull'aria."

COUNTESS:
Come, write what I say, and I take full
responsibility: "Song of the Zephyr."

SUSANNA
"Sull'aria..."

SUSANNA: *(writing)*
"of the Zephyr."

LA CONTESSA
"Che soave zeffiretto..."

COUNTESS:
"How gentle the zephyr..."

SUSANNA:
"Zeffiretto..."

SUSANNA:
"Zephyr..."

LA CONTESSA:
"Questa sera spirerà..."

COUNTESS:
"The night will inspire..."

SUSANNA:
"Questa sera spirerà..."

SUSANNA:
"The night will inspire..."

LA CONTESSA
"Sotto i pini del boschetto."

COUNTESS:
"Under the pine groves."

SUSANNA
"Sotto i pini..."

SUSANNA:
"Under the pines..."

LA CONTESSA
"Sotto i pini del boschetto."

COUNTESS:
"Under the pine groves."

SUSANNA
"Sotto i pini...del boschetto..."

SUSANNA:
"Under the pines...groves..."

LA CONTESSA:
Ei già il resto capirà.

COUNTESS:
Certainly, he'll understand the remainder.

SUSANNA:
Certo, certo il capirà.
Piegato è il foglio. Or come si sigilla?

SUSANNA:
Certainly, certainly he'll understand.
It is folded. Now how is it to be sealed?

LA CONTESSA:
Ecco, prendi una spilla:
Servirà di sigillo.
Attendi, scrivi sul riverso del foglio,
"Rimandate il sigillo."

COUNTESS:
Here, we'll use a pin.
That will serve as a seal.
One moment, write on the back of the letter,
"Send the seal back as an answer."

SUSANNA:
È più bizzarro di quel della patente.

SUSANNA:
He won't forget it like he forgot the seal on the commission.

LA CONTESSA:
Presto nascondi, io sento venir gente.

COUNTESS:
Put it away now. I hear people coming.

Barbarina and peasant girls enter. Cherubino is among them dressed as a peasant girl. All carry bunches of flowers.

CONTADINELLE:
Ricevete, oh padroncina,
queste rose e questi fior,
che abbiam colti stamattina
per mostrarvi il nostro amor.

PEASANT GIRLS:
Noble lady, to show our love,
we offer these roses
and these flowers
that we have gathered this morning.

Siamo tante contadine,
e siam tutte poverine,
ma quel poco che rechiamo
ve lo diamo di buon cor.

We are simple peasants,
and we are all very poor,
but the little that we bring,
we give with a good heart.

BARBARINA:
Queste sono, madama,
le ragazze del loco
che il poco ch'han vi vengono ad offrire,
e vi chiedon perdon del loro ardire.

BARBARINA:
Madame, these are girls from the village. We
hope that you will not refuse these flowers, for
they are all that we can offer you.

LA CONTESSA:
Oh brave, vi ringrazio.

COUNTESS:
I thank you for your kindness.

SUSANNA:
Come sono vezzose.

SUSANNA:
They are so charming.

LA CONTESSA:
E chi è, narratemi, quell'amabil fanciulla
ch'ha l'aria sì modesta?

COUNTESS: *(pointing to Cherubino)*
Tell me, who is that shy and modest girl over
there?

BARBARINA:
Ell'è mia cugina, e per le nozze è venuta ier sera.

LA CONTESSA:
Onoriamo la bella forestiera,
venite qui, datemi i vostri fiori.
Come arrossì. Susanna, e non ti pare
che somigli ad alcuno?

SUSANNA:
Al naturale.

BARBARINA:
She is one of my cousins. She arrived last night to stay with us for the wedding.

COUNTESS:
Then we ought to honor the pretty guest. Come here. Give me your flowers.
How she blushes! Susanna, doesn't she resemble someone?

SUSANNA:
The very image.

The Count enters, followed by Antonio.
Antonio pulls off Cherubino's head-dress and puts on his soldier's hat.

ANTONIO:
Ehi! Cospettaccio! È questi l'uffiziale.

LA CONTESSA:
Oh stelle!

SUSANNA:
(Malandrino!)

IL CONTE:
Ebben, madama!

LA CONTESSA:
Io sono, oh signor mio, irritata e sorpresa al par di voi.

IL CONTE:
Ma stamane?

LA CONTESSA:
Stamane. Per l'odierna festa volevam travestirlo al modo stesso, che l'han vestito adesso.

IL CONTE:
E perché non partiste?

CHERUBINO:
Signor!

IL CONTE:
Saprò punire la sua ubbidienza.

ANTONIO:
Hey! Caught you at last, gallant captain.

COUNTESS:
Oh, heavens!

SUSANNA:
(Little rascal!)

COUNT:
Well, Madame!

COUNTESS:
I must inform your lordship that I am just as surprised as you are.

COUNT:
But this morning?

COUNTESS:
This morning, I admit we intended to dress him in girl's clothes in order to make some fun this evening.

COUNT: *(to Cherubino)*
And why haven't you left?

CHERUBINO:
Sir!

COUNT:
I know how to punish your disobedience.

BARBARINA:
Eccellenza, Eccellenza, voi mi dite sì spesso
qual volta m'abbracciate, e mi baciate:
Barbarina, se m'ami, ti darò quel che brami.

BARBARINA:
Please your lordship. You often said to me when
you visited me, "Barbarina, if you love me I'll
give you anything that you ask for"

IL CONTE:
Io dissi questo?

COUNT:
I said that?

BARBARINA:
Voi. Or datemi , padrone, in sposo Cherubino,
e v'amerò, com'amo il mio gattino.

BARBARINA:
Oh yes your lordship. Now if you give me
Cherubino for a husband, I'll love you like my
little kitten.

LA CONTESSA:
Ebbene: or tocca a voi.

COUNTESS: *(to the Count)*
Well. I think it's your turn.

ANTONIO:
Brava figliuola, hai buon maestro, che ti fa
scuola.

ANTONIO:
Great, little girl, you've had a good teacher for
your lessons.

IL CONTE:
(Non so qual uom, qual demone, qual Dio
rivolga tutto quanto a torto mio.)

COUNT: *(aside)*
(Is it a plot of man, or demon, or God that
makes everything go wrong.)

(Enter Figaro.)

FIGARO:
Signor, se trattenete tutte queste ragazze,
addio feste, addio danza.

FIGARO:
Sir, if you keep these girls waiting, we'll have no
party and no dancing.

IL CONTE:
E che, vorresti ballar col pié stravolto?

COUNT: *(ironically)*
Dancing with your sprained foot?

FIGARO:
Eh, non mi duol più molto.
Andiam, belle fanciulle.

FIGARO::
Oh, it doesn't give me much pain now. Come,
my pretty girls.

LA CONTESSA:
(Come si caverà dall'imbarazzo?)

COUNTESS: *(aside to Susanna)*
(How will he get through this problem?)

SUSANNA:
(Lasciate fare a lui.)

SUSANNA:
(Leave everything to him.)

IL CONTE:
Per buona sorte i vasi eran di creta.

COUNT:
Luckily the pots were made of clay.

FIGARO:
Senza fallo. Andiamo dunque, andiamo.

FIGARO:
Without doubt. Let us go then, let us go.

ANTONIO:
E intanto a cavallo di galoppo a Siviglia
andava il paggio.

ANTONIO:
And in the meantime, the page was galloping
off to Seville.

FIGARO:
Di galoppo, o di passo, buon viaggio.
Venite, oh belle giovani.

IL CONTE:
E a te la sua patente era in tasca rimasta.

FIGARO:
Certamente, che razza di domande!

ANTONIO:
Via, non gli far più motti, ei non t'intende.
Ed ecco chi pretende che sia un bugiardo il
mio signor nipote.

FIGARO:
Cherubino?

ANTONIO:
Or ci sei.

FIGARO
Che diamin canta?

IL CONTE:
Non canta, no, ma dice ch'egli saltò stamane
sui garofani.

FIGARO:
Ei lo dice! Sarà se ho saltato io, si può dare
ch'anch'esso abbia fatto lo stesso.

IL CONTE:
Anch'esso?

FIGARO:
Perché no?
Io non impugno mai quel che non so.
Ecco la marcia, andiamo;
ai vostri posti, oh belle, ai vostri posti.
Susanna, dammi il braccio.

SUSANNA:
Eccolo!

FIGARO:
Gallop or on foot, good journey.
Come, my pretty damsels.

COUNT:
And he left the commission in your pocket.

FIGARO:
Certainly, I can't understand why you ask!

ANTONIO: *(to Susanna)*
No good your making signals. He cannot read
them. Here is a person who maintains that my
future nephew is a liar.

FIGARO:
Cherubino?

ANTONIO:
That's him.

FIGARO: *(to the Count)*
And what does he say?

COUNT:
That this morning it was he who jumped down
from the window on to the flower pots.

FIGARO:
He said that! If I could jump, he is lighter
and could certainly do the same.

COUNT:
You both jumped?

FIGARO:
Why not?
I wouldn't call him a liar.
Here is the march, let us go;
take your places, my beauties.
Susanna, give me your arm.

SUSANNA:
Here it is.

All exit except the Count and Countess.

IL CONTE:
Temerari.

COUNT:
This is shameless.

LA CONTESSA:
Io son di ghiaccio!

COUNTESS:
I am frozen!

IL CONTE:
Contessa!

COUNT:
Countess!

LA CONTESSA:
Or non parliamo. Ecco qui le due nozze,
riceverle dobbiam, alfin si tratta d'una vostra
protetta.
Seggiamo.

COUNTESS:
Let us not speak now. There are two weddings,
and we must receive them. Bear in mind that it
is a protege of yours that is in question. Be
seated.

IL CONTE:
Seggiamo (e meditiam vendetta).

COUNT:
Let us sit down (and think of revenge!)

The Count and Countess are seated. The wedding procession begins: two young girls
bear Susanna's bridal hat and veil. Antonio leads Susanna before the Count; she kneels
and receives the veil from him. Figaro leads Marcellina before the Countess.
The two wedding couples are seated facing the Count and Countess.

DUE DONNE:
Amanti costanti,
seguaci d'onor,
cantate, lodate
sì saggio signor.
A un dritto cedendo,
che oltraggia, che offende,
ei caste vi rende
ai vostri amator.

TWO YOUNG GIRLS:
You constant lovers,
who follow honor,
Do sing, do praise
such a good lord.
He ceded a right,
that was insulting and degrading,
and returns chastity
to lovers.

TUTTI:
Cantiamo, lodiamo sì saggio signor!

ALL:
Let us sing, let us praise so good a lord,

Susanna, while kneeling before the Count, gives him a letter. The Count opens the
letter and pricks his finger with the pin that sealed the letter.

IL CONTE:
Eh già, la solita usanza, le donne ficcan gli
aghi in ogni loco. Ah, ah, capisco il gioco.

COUNT:
(It is the usual custom, women thrust pins
everywhere.) Oh, now I understand the trick!
(He looks for the pin)

FIGARO:
Un biglietto amoroso che gli diè nel passar
qualche galante, ed era sigillato d'una spilla,
ond'ei si punse il dito,

Il Narciso or la cerca; oh, che stordito!

FIGARO: *(aside)*
A love letter? Some lover's friend gave it to
him in passing, and it was sealed with a pin,
which pricked his finger.

The Adonis is now looking for it. Oh, what a
foolish fellow!)

The Count reads the letter, kisses it, finds the pin and puts it on his coat.

IL CONTE:
Andate, amici! E sia per questa sera
disposto l'apparato nuziale
colla più ricca pompa; io vo' che sia
magnifica la feste, e canti e fuochi,
e gran cena, e gran ballo, e ognuno impari
com'io tratto color, che a me son cari.

CORO
Amanti costanti,
seguaci d'onor,
cantate, lodate
sì saggio signor.
A un dritto cedendo,
che oltraggia, che offende,
ei caste vi rende
ai vostri amator.
Cantiamo, lodiamo
sì saggio signor!

COUNT:
Go, friends! And let the nuptial preparations
be ready for tonight, with the richest pomp,
magnificent entertainment, singing, fireworks,
a great dinner, and a grand ball. Let all learn
how I treat those who are dear to me.

CHORUS:
You constant lovers,
who follow honor,
Do sing, do praise
such a good lord.
Who gives up a right,
insulting, degrading,
and return chastely
to your lovers.
We sing and praise
our good lord!

All depart

ACT IV

It is night in a garden leading to the Castle.
Barbarina enters with a lantern. She searches for something on the ground.

BARBARINA:
L'ho perduta, me meschina,
ah, chi sa dove sarà?
Non la trovo. E mia cugina,
e il padron cosa dirà?

BARBARINA: *(searching)*
I have lost it, how dreadful.
Oh, who knows where it is?
What will I say to my poor cousin and my
master?

Figaro and Marcellina enter.

FIGARO:
Barbarina, cos'hai?

FIGARO:
Barbarina, what is the matter?

BARBARINA:
L'ho perduta, cugino.

BARBARINA:
I have lost it, cousin.

FIGARO:
Cosa?

FIGARO:
What?

MARCELLINA:
Cosa?

BARBARINA:
La spilla, che a me diede il padrone
per recar a Susanna.

FIGARO:
A Susanna la spilla?
E così, tenerella, il mestiero già sai,.
di far tutto sì ben quel che tu fai?

BARBARINA:
Cos'è, vai meco in collera?

FIGARO:
E non vedi ch'io scherzo?

MARCELLINA:
What?

BARBARINA:
The pin my master gave me to return to
Susanna.

FIGARO:
A pin to Susanna? So already at your age
you've begun to go running other people's
errands?

BARBARINA:
But why are you so angry?

FIGARO:
Can't you see I was just kidding?

Figaro searches the ground. Then he takes a pin from Marcellina
and gives it to Barbarina.

Osserva. Questa è la spilla che il Conte
da recare ti diede alla Susanna, e servia di
sigillo a un bigliettino; vedi s'io sono istrutto.

BARBARINA:
E perché il chiedi a me quando sai tutto?

FIGARO:
Avea gusto d'udir come il padrone ti die' la
commissione.

BARBARINA:
Che miracoli! "Tieni, fanciulla, reca questa
spilla alla bella Susanna, e dille: Questo
è il sigillo de' pini."

FIGARO:
Ah, ah, de' pini!

BARBARINA:
È ver ch'ei mi soggiunse: "Guarda che alcun
non veda." Ma tu già tacerai.

FIGARO:
Sicuramente.

BARBARINA:
A te già niente preme.

Look. This is the pin the Count gave you to
give back to Susanna, and it was used to seal a
letter. You see how instructive I am.

BARBARINA:
If you know everything, why do you ask me?

FIGARO:
I would like you to tell me why his lordship sent
you on this errand.

BARBARINA:
He just said to me, "Here Barbarina, take this
pin and give it to your cousin Susanna, and tell
her: 'This is the seal of the pinewood.'"

FIGARO:
Oh, the pinewood!

BARBARINA:
But he told me, "Be careful no one sees you."
But you have seen me.

FIGARO:
You can trust me.

BARBARINA:
There's no harm done if you know.

FIGARO:
Oh niente, niente.

BARBARINA:
Addio, mio bel cugino;
vò da Susanna, e poi da Cherubino.

FIGARO
Madre!

MARCELLINA
Figlio!

FIGARO:
Son morto!

MARCELLINA:
Calmati, figlio mio.

FIGARO:
Son morto, dico.

MARCELLINA:
Flemma, flemma, e poi flemma!Il fatto è serio;
e pensarci convien, ma pensa un poco che
ancor non sai di chi prenda gioco.

FIGARO:
Ah, quella spilla, oh madre, è quella stessa che
poc'anzi ei raccolse.

MARCELLINA:
È ver, ma questo al più ti porge un dritto
di stare in guardia, e vivere in sospetto.
Ma non sai, se in effetto.

FIGARO:
All'erta dunque: il loco del congresso
so dov'è stabilito.

MARCELLINA:
Dove vai figlio mio?

FIGARO:
A vendicar tutti i mariti: addio.

FIGARO:
Of course not.

BARBARINA:
Adieu, my handsome cousin. I'll go to
Susanna, and then to Cherubino.
(Barbarina exits.)

FIGARO:
Mother!

MARCELLINA:
 Son!

FIGARO:
I am finished!

MARCELLINA:
Be calm, my son.

FIGARO:
I tell you I'm finished.

MARCELLINA:
Patience, patience, always patience! The
problem is serious and requires careful
thought. Now to begin with, you don't know
who's going to be the victim.

FIGARO:
Oh, that pin is the very same pin which not
long ago he picked up.

MARCELLINA:
True, but this gives only gives you, at most,
cause to be upon your guard and to be
suspicious. You're still uncertain.

FIGARO:
Then, I must be alert. I do know where the
meeting place is.

MARCELLINA:
Where are you going, son?

FIGARO:
To avenge all husbands. Farewell!

Figaro departs.

MARCELLINA:
Presto avvertiam Susanna:
io la credo innocente: quella faccia,
quell'aria di modestia, è caso ancora
ch'ella non fosse, ah quando il cor non ciurma
personale interesse, ogni donna è portata alla
difesa del suo povero sesso,
da questi uomini ingrati a torto oppresso.

Il capro e la capretta
son sempre in amistà,
l'agnello all'agnelletta
la guerra mai non fa.
Le più feroci belve
per selve e per campagne
lascian le lor compagne
in pace e libertà.
Sol noi povere femmine
che tanto amiam questi uomini,
trattate siam dai perfidi
ognor con crudeltà!

MARCELLINA:
I must quickly warn Susanna because I believe
she is innocent; that face and
modest air are reasons enough.
I have no reason to be jealous anymore. Surely
all women ought to protect each other. It is our
duty because we so maltreated by our
husbands and lovers.

The goat and the billy-goat are always
companions.
With the lamb and the lambkin
the battle never ends.
The most ferocious beasts
in the fields and the forests,
grant their partners
peace and freedom to live.
Only the poor women
who love these men so much,
are treated with treachery
and always with cruelty.

Marcellina exits

A Garden. There are pines surrounding two Pavilions.
Barberina, Figaro, Bartolo, Basilio and some ruffians enter.

BARBARINA:
Nel padiglione a manca: ei così disse:
è questo, è questo, e poi se non venisse!

Oh ve' che brava gente! A stento darmi
un arancio, una pera, e una ciambella.
"Per chi madamigella?
Oh, per qualcun, signori:
già lo sappiam: ebbene!"
il padron l'odia, ed io gli voglio bene,
però costommi un bacio, e cosa importa,
forse qualcun me'l renderà.

Son morta!

BARBARINA:
I think he said the pavilion on the left. It must be
this one, but what if he doesn't come?

These people are so awful! I could hardly get
them to give me an orange or a biscuit: "Who is
it for?
Oh, it's for a friend
Well, we thought as much!"
His lordship hates him, and I love him. I paid a
kiss for this, but what does it matter. Perhaps
someone will pay it back.

(She sees Figaro and then leaves)
Oh mercy!

FIGARO:
È Barbarina chi va là?

FIGARO:
Is that Barbarina over there?

BASILIO:
Son quelli che invitasti a venir.

BASILIO:
We are the men you invited to come.

BARTOLO:
Che brutto ceffo! Sembri un cospirator. Che diamin sono quegli infausti apparati?

FIGARO:
Lo vedrete tra poco. In questo loco celebrerem la festa della mia sposa onesta e del feudal signor.

BASILIO:
(Ah, buono, buono, capisco come egli è, accordati si son senza di me.)

FIGARO:
Voi da questi contorni non vi scostate; intanto io vado a dar certi ordini, e torno in pochi istanti.
A un fischio mio correte tutti quanti.

BASILIO:
Ha i diavoli nel corpo.

BARTOLO:
Ma cosa nacque?

BASILIO:
Nulla. Susanna piace al Conte; ella d'accordo gli die' un appuntamento che a Figaro non piace.

BARTOLO:
E che, dunque dovria soffrirlo in pace?

BASILIO:
Quel che soffrono tanti ei soffrir non potrebbe? E poi sentite, che guadagno può far? Nel mondo, amico, l'accozzarla co' grandi fu pericolo ognora:
dan novanta per cento e han vinto ancora.

In quegl'anni, in cui val poco la mal pratica ragion, ebbi anch'io lo stesso foco, fui quel pazzo ch'or non son.
Che col tempo e coi perigli, donna flemma capitò; e i capricci, ed i puntigli della testa mi cavò.

BARTOLO: *(to Figaro)*
What an ugly face! You look like a conspirator. (Who are those devilish looking ones?)

FIGARO:
You'll see very shortly. You are invited to witness the ancient privilege of the lord of the manor granted by my virtuous wife.

BASILIO:
(Oh, great! I understand they have agreed without me.)

FIGARO: *(to the ruffians)*
Do not go far from here. Meanwhile I'll make certain arrangements, and I'll be back in a moment.
When I whistle all of you run!
(Figaro leaves.)

BASILIO:
He's possessed by the devil.

BARTOLO:
But what is it that has deranged him?

BASILIO:
Nothing. Susanna likes the Count. She is consenting to a meeting that Figaro does not like.

BARTOLO:
Is he supposed to bear it peacefully?

BASILIO:
Many a man has likewise suffered, so why should he object? And consider what he can gain? In this world it was always dangerous to oppose the great; they give very little and always win.

When I was young and inexperienced, I used emotion rather than reason.
I too had the same great fire;
I was a madman, but no more.
Time has brought me an understanding of the wiles and caprices of women, and in my mind, I have overcome their stubbornness.

Presso un piccolo abituro
seco lei mi trasse un giorno,
e togliendo giù dal muro
del pacifico soggiorno
una pella di somaro,
prendi disse, oh figlio caro,
poi disparve, e mi lasciò.

One day she took me to
a humble dwelling place,
And then from the wall of the peaceful abode she took down
the skin of an old ass;
take this, said, dear son,
and then she left me and disappeared.

Mentre ancor tacito
guardo quel dono,
il ciel s'annuvola
rimbomba il tuono,
mista alla grandine
scroscia la piova,
ecco le membra
coprir mi giova
col manto d'asino
che mi donò.

While I quieted down,
I looked at the gift.
The clouds came on,
and I heard the roar of thunder,
and hail and rain
poured all around.
I therefore found it good
to cover myself
with the mantle of the
ass she gave me.

Finisce il turbine,
nè fo due passi
che fiera orribile
dianzi a me fassi;
già già mi tocca
l'ingorda bocca,
già di difendermi
speme non ho.

The storm ceased.
I went on a little;
I saw a wild beast
rushing toward me;
I saw his mouth
and his voracious looks.
Any hopes to defend
myself were futile.

Ma il finto ignobile
del mio vestito
tolse alla belva
sì l'appetito,
che disprezzandomi
si rinselvò.
Così conoscere
mi fè la sorte,
ch'onte, pericoli,
vergogna, e morte
col cuoio d'asino
fuggir si può.

But the humble scent
of my clothes,
cured the appetite
of the beast,
who despised me,
but ran into the woods.
Thus I learned
about my fate:
that disgrace, danger,
shame, and death,
may be avoided
with the skin of an ass.

All depart, and then Figaro appears..

FIGARO:
Tutto è disposto: l'ora dovrebbe esser vicina; io sento gente. È dessa, non è alcun, buia è la notte, ed io comincio omai, a fare il scimunito mestiero di marito.

FIGARO:
All is prepared: the hour ought to be near. I hear someone. It's her. No, it is no one. The night is full and I begin now to play the silly role of a husband!

Ingrata! Nel momento della mia cerimonia ei godeva leggendo, e nel vederlo io rideva di me, senza saperlo.

Ungrateful woman! At the ceremony, he was enjoying what he read, and I saw him and laughed without knowing why!

Oh Susanna, Susanna, quanta pena mi costi, con
quell'ingenua faccia, con quegli occhi
innocenti,chi creduto l'avria?
Ah, che il fidarsi a donna è ognor follia.

O Susanna! Susanna! What anguish you have
cost me, with your air of sincerity and those
innocent eyes. Who could have believed it?-
Trusting a woman is a great folly!

Moderato
FIGARO

A-pri - te un po' quegl'occhi,   uomini incauti a schiocchi,

Aprite un po' quegl'occhi,
uomini incauti e sciocchi,
guardate queste femmine,
guardate cosa son!

Open your eyes a little,
imprudent and foolish men;
look at these women,
and see what they really are!

Queste chiamate Dee
dagli ingannati sensi
a cui tributa incensi
la debole ragion.

These are called goddesses
 by those whose senses are deceived,
and who raise altars to them
by the weakness of their reason.

Son streghe che incantano
per farci penar,
sirene che cantano
per farci affogar,
civette che allettano
per trarci le piume,
comete che brillano
per toglierci il lume;
son rose spinose,
son volpi vezzose,
son orse benigne,
colombe maligne,
maestre d'inganni,
amiche d'affanni
che fingono, mentono.

They are witches that bewitch,
to put us to torment;
sirens who sing
but to drown us;
owls who ensnare us
to pick our feathers;
comets which shine
to dazzle and blind us;
they are roses full of thorns,
they are beautiful foxes;
they are kind bears,
wicked doves;
skillful in fraud,
creatures of sorrow,
who pretend and lie.

Amore non senton,
non senton pietà,
no, no, no, no!
Il resto nol dico,
già ognun lo sa!

They feel neither love
nor pity.
No, no, no!
I need say no more,
for every one knows it!

The Countess and Susanna enter, disguised in each other's clothes.
Marcellina and Figaro are seen walking about.

SUSANNA:
Signora, ella mi disse che Figaro verravvi.

SUSANNA:
Madam, you told me that Figaro would come.

MARCELLINA:
Anzi è venuto. Abbassa un po' la voce.

MARCELLINA:
He is here. Speak softly.

SUSANNA:
Dunque, un ci ascolta, e l'altro dee venir a cercarmi, incominciam.

SUSANNA:
Then one hears us, and the other comes to seek me. Let's begin.

MARCELLINA:
Io voglio qui celarmi.

MARCELLINA:
I will conceal myself here.

SUSANNA:
Madama, voi tremate; avreste freddo?

SUSANNA: *(to the Countess)*
Madame, you tremble; are you cold?

LA CONTESSA:
Parmi umida la notte; io mi ritiro.

COUNTESS:
I think it is a damp night: I'm leaving.

Figaro appears.

FIGARO:
(Eccoci della crisi al grande istante.)

FIGARO:
We are now at the great critical moment!

Figaro strolls around, withdraws, and the immediately reappears.

SUSANNA:
Io sotto questi piante, se madama il permette, resto prendere il fresco una mezz'ora.

SUSANNA:
If your ladyship allows me, I prefer to stay here and take in the fresh air of the pine trees.

FIGARO:
Il fresco! Il fresco!

FIGARO:
The air, among the pinetrees!

LA CONTESSA:
Restaci in buon'ora.

COUNTESS: *(from hiding)*
We'll rest an hour.

SUSANNA:
Il birbo è in sentinella.
Divertiamci anche noi,
diamogli la mercè de' dubbi suoi.

SUSANNA:
That rascal is on the watch.
We'll also create a diversion, and pay him for daring to suspect me.

Giunse alfin il momento
che godrò senz'affanno
in braccio all'idol mio.
Timide cure, uscite dal mio petto,
a turbar non venite il mio diletto!

At last the moment has come
that I shall have pleasure without sorrow in the arms of my beloved.
Timid apprehensions, begone from my breast,
and do not disturb my happiness!

Oh, come par che all'amoroso foco
l'amenità del loco,
la terra e il ciel risponda,
come la notte i furti miei seconda!

Oh, how there is such an amorous spirit here;
the earth and the sky respond to my amorous wishes! How the night favors my secret love!

Andante
SUSANNA

Deh vie - ni, non tar - dar,   o gio - ja bel - la,

Deh, vieni, non tardar, oh gioia bella,
vieni ove amore per goder t'appella,
finché non splende in ciel notturna face,
finché l'aria è ancor bruna e il mondo tace.

Qui mormora il ruscel, qui scherza l'aura,
che col dolce sussurro il cor ristaura,
qui ridono i fioretti e l'erba è fresca,
ai piaceri d'amor qui tutto adesca.
Vieni, ben mio, tra queste piante ascose,
ti vo' la fronte incoronar di rose.

Then come, do not delay, my dearest jewel.
Come where love invites your pleasure. Come,
while the stars of night shine in the sky,
darkness reigns, and the world is wrapped in
silence.

The brook murmurs, the zephyrs play, and
their sweet sounds comfort the heart.
Here little flowers seem to smile, and the fresh
grass invites us all to love. Oh, come, my love,
and I will encircle you head with roses.

Susanna withdraws among the trees.

FIGARO:
Perfida, e in quella forma ella meco mentia?
Non so s'io veglio, o dormo.

FIGARO:
False woman, who has lied to me? I don't
know whether I am awake or asleep!

CHERUBINO:
La la la...

CHERUBINO:
La, la, la,...

LA CONTESSA:
Il picciol paggio.

COUNTESS:
It's the little page.

CHERUBINO:
Io sento gente, entriamo ove entrò Barbarina.
Oh, vedo qui una donna.

CHERUBINO:
I hear people about, I'll go where Barbarina
went! Oh, I see a woman over there.

LA CONTESSA:
Ahi, me meschina!

COUNTESS:
Alas, I am finished!

CHERUBINO:
M'inganno, a quel cappello,
che nell'ombra vegg'io parmi Susanna.

CHERUBINO:
Am I mistaken? That hat! In the dark, I think it
is Susanna.

LA CONTESSA:
E se il Conte ora vien, sorte tiranna!

COUNTESS:
It would be a cruel fate if the Count should
come now!

CHERUBINO:
Pian pianin le andrò più presso,
tempo perso non sarà.

CHERUBINO: *(approaches her)*
Quietly, I'll approach her, and not lose any time.

LA CONTESSA:
(Ah, se il Conte arriva adesso qualche
imbroglio accaderà!)

COUNTESS:
(Oh, if the Count should come now, something
awful will happen.

CHERUBINO:
Susanetta! Non risponde?
Colla mano il volto asconde,
or la burlo, in verità.

CHERUBINO: *(to the Countess)*
Dear Susanna? She doesn't answer.
I'll indeed catch her now.
(Cherubino kisses her hand.)

LA CONTESSA:
Arditello, sfacciatello,
ite presto via di qua!

COUNTESS:
This is shameless, impudent fellow, get away
from here immediately.

CHERUBINO:
Smorfiosa, maliziosa,
io già so perché sei qua!

CHERUBINO:
So shy, and just to tease me.
I know why you are here!

The Count and Figaro appear.

IL CONTE:
Ecco qui la mia Susanna!

COUNT:
There she is, my Susanna!

SUSANNA e FIGARO:
Ecco qui l'uccellatore.

SUSANNA and FIGARO:
Here's the amorous pursuer.

CHERUBINO
Non far meco la tiranna!

CHERUBINO: *(to the Countess)*
Don't be so hard on me!

SUSANNA, IL CONTE, FIGARO:
Ah, nel sen mi batte il core!
Un altr'uom con lei sta; alla voce è quegli il
paggio.

SUSANNA, COUNT, FIGARO:
Look how the heart beats!
There's another man. By the sound of his
voice, it is the page.

LA CONTESSA:
Via partite, o chiamo gente!

COUNTESS:
Go, or I'll call for help!

CHERUBINO:
Dammi un bacio, o non fai niente.

CHERUBINO:
Give me a kiss, or do nothing.

LA CONTESSA:
Anche un bacio, che coraggio!

COUNTESS:
Again a kiss. What impertinence!

CHERUBINO:
E perché far io non posso,
quel che il Conte ognor farà?

CHERUBINO:
And why do you refuse what the Count gets
every day?

SUSANNA, LA CONTESSA, IL CONTE,
FIGARO:
Temerario!

SUSANNA, COUNTESS, COUNT,
FIGARO:
What effrontery!

CHERUBINO:
Oh ve', che smorfie!
Sai ch'io fui dietro il sofà.

CHERUBINO:
Oh why are you so prudish! You know I was
behind the sofa.

SUSANNA, LA CONTESSA, IL CONTE, FIGARO:
Se il ribaldo ancor sta saldo la faccenda guasterà.

CHERUBINO:
Prendi intanto!

SUSANNA, COUNTESS, COUNT, FIGARO:
If he remains here, he'll spoil our little game.

CHERUBINO: *(about to kiss her)*
Take a kiss then!

The Count steps between them, and receives the kiss from Cherubino.

LA CONTESSA, CHERUBINO:
Oh cielo, il Conte!

COUNTESS, CHERUBINO:
Oh heavens, the Count!

The Count, attempts to box Cherubino's ears, but he leaves quickly, and Figaro is hit instead.

FIGARO:
Vo' veder cosa fan là.

FIGARO:
I must see what's going on.

IL CONTE:
Perché voi nol ripetete, ricevete questo qua!

COUNT:
I will teach you better manners, so that you'll finally be gone from here.

FIGARO, SUSANNA, LA CONTESSA:
Ah, ci ho/ha fatto un bel guadagno colla mia/sua curiosità!

FIGARO, SUSANNA, COUNTESS:
That's his reward. He was rash to interfere!

IL CONTE:
Ah, ci ha fatto un bel guadagno colla sua temerità!

COUNT:
That's his rewarded. He was rash to interfere!

FIGARO e SUSANNA:
Partito è alfin l'audace, accostati ben mio!

FIGARO and SUSANNA:
Thank goodness he's departed. Come closer to me!

LA CONTESSA:
Giacché così vi piace, eccomi qui signor.

COUNTESS:
I am here my lord. What would please you?

FIGARO:
Che compiacente femmina! Che sposa di buon cor!

FIGARO:
What obliging women! What a good-hearted woman!

IL CONTE:
Porgimi la manina!

COUNT:
Give me your hand!

LA CONTESSA:
Io ve la dò.

COUNTESS:
My hand is yours.

IL CONTE:
Carina!

COUNT:
My dearest!

FIGARO:
Carina!

FIGARO:
My dearest!

IL CONTE:
Che dita tenerelle, che delicata pelle,
mi pizzica, mi stuzzica, m'empie d'un nuovo
ardor.

SUSANNA, LA CONTESSA, FIGARO:
La cieca prevenzione delude la ragione
inganna i sensi ognor.

IL CONTE:
Oltre la dote, oh cara, ricevi anco un brillante
che a te porge un amante
in pegno del suo amor.

LA CONTESSA:
Tutto Susanna piglia dal suo benefattor.

SUSANNA, IL CONTE, FIGARO:
Va tutto a maraviglia, ma il meglio manca
ancor.

LA CONTESSA:
Signor, d'accese fiaccole io veggio il balenar.

IL CONTE:
Entriam, mia bella Venere, andiamoci a celar!

SUSANNA, FIGARO:
Mariti scimuniti, venite ad imparar!

LA CONTESSA:
Al buio, signor mio?

IL CONTE:
È quello che vogl'io.
Tu sai che là per leggere io non desio d'entrar.

SUSANNA e LA CONTESSA:
I furbi sono in trappola, comincia ben l'affar.

FIGARO
La perfida lo seguita, è vano il dubitar.

IL CONTE:
Chi passa?

FIGARO:
Passa gente!

LA CONTESSA:
È Figaro; men vò!

COUNT:
How soft your hand, and what delicate hair; it
stings me, arouses me, and fills me with new
ardor.

SUSANNA, COUNTESS, FIGARO:
Amorous passion deludes reason and deceives
all senses.

COUNT:
You have received a dowry, but let me give
you this ring as a token of my eternal love.

COUNTESS:
Susanna takes everything from her benefactor.

SUSANNA, COUNT, FIGARO:
Our plot is marvelous, but it must proceed
faster.

COUNTESS: *(to the Count)*
My lord, I see torchlight approaching in the
distance.

COUNT:
Let's enter here and hide, my beautiful Venus!

SUSANNA, FIGARO:
Here's a lesson for idiotic husbands to learn.

COUNTESS:
Isn't it dark, my lord?

COUNT:
That's what I want.
You know that I'm not going in there to read.

SUSANNA, COUNTESS:
Both our men are in the trap. The work goes well.

FIGARO:
I followed the betrayer, it is vain to doubt.

COUNT:
Who is there?

FIGARO:
People pass!

COUNTESS:
It is Figaro. I think I'll leave.

IL CONTE:
Andate; io poi verrò.

COUNT:
Let's go.

The Countess goes in to one Pavillion door, the Count into the other.

FIGARO:
Tutto è tranquillo e placido;
entrò la bella Venere;
col vago Marte a prendere
nuovo Vulcan del secolo
in rete la potrò.

FIGARO:
It is quiet and tranquil here.
The fair Venus has gone,
with her beloved Mars.
As a Vulcan of these times,
I'll catch her in my net.
(Susanna enters.)

SUSANNA:
Ehi, Figaro, tacete.

SUSANNA:
Hey Figaro, be quiet.

FIGARO:
(Oh, questa è la Contessa.)
A tempo qui giungete, vedrete là voi stessa, il
Conte, e la mia sposa,
di propria man la cosa toccar io vi farò.

FIGARO:
(Oh, it is the Countess.)
You've come at the right time. You yourself
will see the Count and my bride. I'll convince
you with your own eyes.

SUSANNA:
Parlate un po' più basso, di qua non muovo il
passo, ma vendicar mi vò.

SUSANNA:
Speak softer/ will not take a step,
but wish to be avenged.

FIGARO:
(Susanna!) Vendicarsi?

FIGARO:
(Susanna!) Avenged?

SUSANNA:
Sì.

SUSANNA:
Yes.

FIGARO:
Come potria farsi?

FIGARO:
How can you do that?

SUSANNA:
(L'iniquo io vo' sorprendere,
poi so quel che farò.)

SUSANNA:
(I will surprise the villain; then I know what I
will do.)

FIGARO:
(La volpe vuol sorprendermi,
e secondarla vò.)
Ah se madama il vuole!

FIGARO:
(The fox wants to surprise me, and I will
assist.)
Whatever Madame wishes!

SUSANNA:
Su via, manco parole.

SUSANNA:
So now, no talking.

FIGARO:
Eccomi a' vostri piedi, ho pieno il cor di foco,
esaminate il loco, pensate al traditor.

FIGARO:
Here at your feet my heart is afire, think how
you were betrayed.

SUSANNA:
(Come la man mi pizzica, che smania, che
furor!)

FIGARO:
(Come il polmon mi s'altera,
che smania, che calor!)

SUSANNA:
E senz'alcun affetto?

FIGARO:
Suppliscavi il dispetto. Non perdiam tempo
invano, datemi un po' la mano.

SUSANNA:
Servitevi, signor.

FIGARO:
Che schiaffo!

SUSANNA:
Che schiaffo, e questo, e questo, e ancora
questo, e questo, e poi quest'altro.

FIGARO:
Non batter così presto.

SUSANNA:
E questo, signor scaltro, e questo, e poi
quest'altro ancor.

FIGARO:
O schiaffi graziosissimi, oh, mio felice amor.

SUSANNA:
Impara, impara, oh perfido, a fare il seduttor.

FIGARO:
Pace, pace, mio dolce tesoro,
io conobbi la voce che adoro
e che impressa ognor serbo nel cor.

SUSANNA:
La mia voce?

FIGARO:
La voce che adoro.

SUSANNA e FIGARO:
Pace, pace, mio dolce tesoro,
pace, pace, mio tenero amor.

SUSANNA:
(How my hand urges me, what frenzy, what
rage!)

FIGARO:
How my breath in raised, what frenzy, what
heat!

SUSANNA:
And without some adoration?

FIGARO:
I am disposed to supplicate myself.
Let's not lose time in vain. Give me your hand.

SUSANNA:
Take it, my lord.

FIGARO: *(Susanna slaps him)*
What a slap!

SUSANNA:
What a slap, and this, and this, and another,
and another.

FIGARO:
Stop hitting me.

SUSANNA:
And this, Mr. smart one, and this, and another.

FIGARO:
Oh gracious beating, oh, my happy love.

SUSANNA:
Oh betrayer, learn, learn the fate of a seductor.

FIGARO:
Peace, peace, my sweet treasure. I recognized
your voice, the voice I adore that is etched in
my heart.

SUSANNA:
My voice?

FIGARO:
The voice I adore.

SUSANNA, FIGARO:
Peace, peace, my tender love.
Peace, peace, my tender love.

The Count enters.

IL CONTE:
Non la trovo e girai tutto il bosco.

COUNT:
I can't find her and I've looked all over.

SUSANNA, FIGARO:
(Questi è il Conte, alla voce il conosco.)

SUSANNA, FIGARO:
It is the Count. I recognize his voice.)

IL CONTE:
Ehi, Susanna, sei sorda.sei muta?

COUNT:
Here, Susanna, are you deaf or dumb?

SUSANNA
Bella, bella! Non l'ha conosciuta.

SUSANNA:
Beautiful! He didn't recognize her.

FIGARO:
Chi?

FIGARO:
Who?

SUSANNA:
Madama!

SUSANNA:
Madame!

FIGARO:
Madama?

FIGARO:
Madame?

SUSANNA:
Madama!
La commedia, idol mio, terminiamo,
consoliamo il bizzarro amator!

SUSANNA:
Madame!.
My dear, the play ends. Let's console the
bizarre lover!

FIGARO:
Sì, madama, voi siete il ben mio!

FIGARO: *(kneels before Susanna)*
Yes, noble lady, be mine!

IL CONTE:
La mia sposa! Ah, senz'arme son io.

COUNT:
My wife! Oh, and I am unarmed.

FIGARO:
Un ristoro al mio cor concedete.

FIGARO:
Agree to come back to my heart.

SUSANNA:
Io son qui, faccio quel che volete.

SUSANNA:
I am yours, do what you want.

IL CONTE:
Ah, ribaldi!

COUNT:
Traitors!

SUSANNA e FIGARO:
Ah, corriamo, mio bene, e le pene compensi il
piacer.

SUSANNA, FIGARO:
Let's hasten, and make up for the pains of the
past.

As Susanna and Figaro try to leave, the Count seizes Figaro.

IL CONTE:
Gente, gente, all'armi, all'armi!

COUNT:
Men, bring arms!

FIGARO:
Il padrone!

IL CONTE:
Gente, gente, aiuto, aiuto!

FIGARO:
Son perduto!

**BASILIO,CURZIO, BARTOLO,
ANTONIO:**
Cosa avvenne?

IL CONTE:
Il scellerato m'ha tradito, m'ha infamato
e con chi state a veder!

**BASILIO,CURZIO, BARTOLO,
ANTONIO:**
Son stordito, son sbalordito, non mi par che
ciò sia ver!

FIGARO:
Son storditi, son sbalorditi, oh che scena, che
piacer!

IL CONTE:
Invan resistete, uscite, madama,
il premio or avrete di vostra onestà!

FIGARO:
His lordship!

COUNT:
Men, men, help, help!

FIGARO:
I'm finished!

**BASILIO,CURZIO, BARTOLO,
ANTONIO:**
What's happening?

COUNT:
The scoundrel has betrayed me, and you shall
soon see with whom!

**BASILIO,CURZIO, BARTOLO,
ANTONIO:**
I'm astounded, confounded, it just can't be!

FIGARO:
I'm astounded, confounded, and what a
pleasant scene.

COUNT:
To resist is in vain. Come out Madame, and
receive the reward for your honesty!

In succession, Cherubino, Barbarina and Marcellina exit the Pavillion.

Il paggio!

ANTONIO:
Mia figlia!

FIGARO:
Mia madre!

BASILIO, ANTONIO e FIGARO:
Madama!

IL CONTE:
Scoperta è la trama, la perfida è qua.

SUSANNA:
Perdono! Perdono!

The page!

ANTONIO:
My daughter!

FIGARO:
My mother!

BASILIO, ANTONIO, FIGARO:
Madame!

COUNT:
The plot is discovered, and here's the traitor.

SUSANNA:
Forgive me! Forgive me!

IL CONTE:
No, no, non sperarlo.

FIGARO:
Perdono! Perdono!

IL CONTE:
No, no, non vo' darlo!

**BARTOLO, CHERUBINO,
MARCELLINA, BASILIO,
ANTONIO, SUSANNA e FIGARO:**
Perdono! Perdono!

IL CONTE:
No, no, no!

LA CONTESSA:
Almeno io per loro perdono otterrò.

BASILIO, IL CONTE e ANTONIO:
Oh cielo, che veggio!
Deliro! Vaneggio!
Che creder non so?

IL CONTE:
Contessa, perdono!

LA CONTESSA:
Più docile io sono, e dico di sì.

TUTTI
Ah, tutti contenti saremo così.
Questo giorno di tormenti,
di capricci, e di follia,
in contenti e in allegria
solo amor può terminar.

Sposi, amici, al ballo, al gioco,
alle mine date foco!
Ed al suon di lieta marcia
corriam tutti a festeggiar!

COUNT:
No, no, I renounce you.

FIGARO:
Forgive her! Forgive her!

COUNT:
No, no, I won't do it!

**BARTOLO, CHERUBINO,
MARCELLINA, BASILIO,
ANTONIO, SUSANNA e FIGARO:**
Forgive her! Forgive her!

COUNT;
No, no, no!

COUNTESS:
I will then intercede for their forgiveness.

BASILIO, COUNT, ANTONIO:
Oh heavens! What do I see!
A vision! A delusion!
I don't believe what I see?

COUNT:
Countess, forgive me!

COUNTESS:
I forgive you again. I can't say no to you.

ALL:
And so we are all content.
This tumultuous day
 of caprices and folly,
and full of joy,
can only end with love.

Spouses, friends, to the ball, to fun,
and to the fires of passion!
Let's march to the happy beat and the sounds
of celebration!

THE MARRIAGE OF FIGARO

Discography

1934	Henderson (Count); Rautawaara Countess); Mildmay (Susanna);
Domgraf-Fassbaender (Figaro); Helletsgrüber (Cherubino); Willis (Marcellina);
Nash (Basilio); Tajo (Bartolo); Radford (Barbarina);
Glyndebourne Festival Chorus and Orchestra;
Busch (Conductor)

1938	Ahlersmayer (Count); Teschemacher (Countess); Cebotari (Susanna);
Schöffler (Figaro); Kolniak (Cherubino); Waldenau (Marcellina); Vessely (Basilio);
Böhme (Bartolo); Frank (Barbarina);
Stuttgart Radio Chorus and Orchestra;
Böhm (Conductor)

1940	Brownlee (Count); Rethberg (Countess); Albanese (Susanna);
Pinza (Figaro); Jarmila-Novotna (Cherubino); Petina (Marcellina);
De Paolis (Basilio); Baccaloni (Bartolo); Farell (Barbarina);
Metropolitan Opera Chorus and Orchestra;
Panizza (Conductor)

1950	London (Count); Schwartzkopf (Countess); Seefried (Susanna);
Kunz (Figaro); Jurinac (Cherubino); Höngen (Marcellina);
Majkut (Basilio); Rus (Bartolo); Schwaiger (Barbarina);
Vienna State Opera Orchestra and Chorus;
Karajan (Conductor)

1951	Bruscantini (Count); Gatti (Countess); Noni (Susanna); Tajo (Figaro);
Gardino (Cherubino); Truccato-Pace (Marcellina); Mercuriali (Basilio);
Corena (Bartolo); Sciutti (Barbarina);
Milan Radio Chorus and Orchestra;
Previtali (Conductor)

1953	Schöffler (Count); Schwartzkopf (Countess); Seefried (Susanna);
Kunz (Figaro); Gueden (Cherubino); Wagner (Marcellina); Klein (Basilio);
Koréh (Bartolo); Maikl (Barbarina);
Vienna State Opera Chorus/Vienna Philharmonic Orchestra;
Furtwängler (Conductor)

1954	Petri (Count); Schwartzkopf (Countess); Seefried (Susanna); Panerai (Figaro);
Jurinac (Cherubino); Villa (Marcellina); Pirino (Basilio); Maionica (Bartolo);
Adani (Barbarina);
La Scala Chorus and Orchestra;
Karajan (Conductor)

1955	Poell (Count); Della Casa (Countess); Gueden (Susanna); Siepi (Figaro);
Danco (Cherubino); Rössi-Majdan (Marcellina); Dickie (Basilio);
Corena (Bartolo); Felbermayer (Barbarina);
Vienna State Opera Chorus/Vienna Philharmonic Orchestra;
Kleiber (Conductor)

1955	Calabreses (Count); Jurinac (Countess); Sciutti (Susanna);
Bruscantini (Figaro); Stevens (Cherubino); Sinclair (Marcellina);
Cuénod (Basilio); Wallace (Basilio); Sinclair (Barbarina);
Glyndebourne Festival Chorus and Orchestra;
Gui (Conductor)

1955   Rehfuss (Count); Stich-Randall (Countess); Streich (Susanna);
        Panerai (Figaro); Lorengar (Cherubino); Gayraud (Marcellina);
        Cuénod (Basilio); Cortis (Bartolo); Ignal (Barbarina);
        Aix-en-Provence Festival Chorus/Paris Conservatoire Orchestra; Rosbaud (Conductor)

1956   Schöffler (Count); Jurinac (Countess); Streich (Susanna); Berry (Figaro);
        Ludwig (Cherubino); Malaniuk (Marcellina); Majkut (Basilio);
        Czerwenka (Bartolo);
        Vienna State Opera Chorus and Orchestra; Böhm (Conductor)

1959   London (Count); Della Casa (Countess); Peters (Susanna); Tozzi (Figaro);
        Elias (Cherubino); Warfield (Marcellina); Carelli (Basilio); Corena (Bartolo);
        Felbermayer (Barbarina);
        Vienna State Opera Chorus and Orchestra; Leinsdorf (Conductor)

1959   Wächter (Count); Schwartzkopf (Countess); Moffo (Susanna);
        Taddei (Figaro); Cossotto (Cherubino); Gatta (Maarcellina); Ercolani (Basilio);
        Vinco (Bartolo); Fusco (Barbarina);
        Philharmonia Chorus and Orchestra; Giulini (Conductor)

1960   Fischer-Dieskau (Count); Stader (Countess); Seefried (Susanna);
        Capecchi (Figaro); Töpper (Cherubino); Benningsen (Marcellina);
        Kuen (Basilio); Sardi (Bartolo); Schwaiger (Barbarina);
        Berlin RIAS Chorus/Berlin Radio State Orchestra; Fricsay (Conductor)

1964   (in German) Prey (Count); Gueden (Countess); Rothenberger (Susanna);
        Berry (Figaro); Mathis (Cherubino); Burmeister (Marcellina);
        Schreier (Basilio); Ollendorf (Bartolo); Rönisch (Barbarina);
        Dresden State Opera Chorus and Orchestra; Suitner (Conductor)

1967   Fischer-Dieskau (Count); Janowitz (Countess); Mathis (Susanna);
        Prey (Figaro); Troyanos (Cherubino); Johnson (Marcellina);
        Wohlfahrt (Basilio); Lagger (Bartolo); Vogel (Barbarina);
        German Opera Chorus and Orchestra; Böhm (Conductor)

1970   Wixell (Count); Norman (Countess); Freni (Susanna); Ganzarolli (Figaro);
        Minton (Cherubino); Casula (Marcellina); Tear (Basilio); Grant (Bartolo);
        Watson (Barbarina);
        BBC Chorus and Orchestra; Davis (Conductor)

1970   Bacquier (Count); Söderström (Countess); Grist (Susanna); Evans (Figaro);
        Berganza (Cherubino); Burmeister (Marcellina); Hollweg (Basilio);
        Langdon (Bartolo); Price (Barbarina);
        Alldis Choir/New Philharmonia Orchestra; Klemperer (Conductor)

1976   Fischer-Dieskau (Count); Harper (Countess); Blegen (Susanna);
        Evans (Figaro); Berganza (Cherubino); Finnilä (Marcellina);
        Fryatt (Basilio); McCue (Bartolo); Gale (Barbarina);
        Alldis Choir/English Chamber Orchestra; Barenboim (Conductor)

1979   Krause (Count); Tomova-Sintow (Countess); Cortrubas (Susanna);
            Van Dam (Figaro); Von Stade (Cherubino); Berbié (Marcellina);
            Zednik (Basilio); Bastin (Bartolo); Barbaux (Barbarina);
            Vienna State Opera Chorus and Orchestra; Karajan (Conductor)

1981   Allen (Count); Te Kanawa (Countess); Popp (Susanna); Ramey (Figaro);
            Von Stade (Cherubino); Berbié (Marcellina); Tear (Basilio);
            Moll (Bartolo); Kenny (Barbarina);
            London Opera Chorus/London Philharmonic Orchestra; Solti (Conductor)

1986   Raimondi (Count); Popp (Countess); Hendricks (Susanna);
            Van Dam (Figaro); Baltsa (Cherubino); Palmer (Marcellina);
            Baldin (Basilio); Lloyd (Bartolo); Pope (Barbarina);
            Ambrosian Opera Chorus/Academy St. Martin in the Fields Orchestra;
            Marriner (Conductor)

1987   Hynninen (Count); M. Price (Countess); Battle (Susanna); Allen (Figaro);
            Murray (Cherubino); Nicolesco (Marcellina); Ramirez (Basilio);
            Rydl (Bartolo); Pace (Barbarina);
            Vienna State Opera Chorus and Orchestra; Muti (Conductor)

1988   Stilwell (Count); Lott (Countess); Rolandi (Susanna); Desderi (Figaro);
            Esham (Cherubino); Mason (Marcellina); Benelli (Basilio);
            Korn (Bartolo); Dawson (Barbarina);
            Glyndebourne Chorus/London Philharmonic Orchestra; Haitink (Conductor)

1988   Hagegard (Count); Augér (Countess); Bonney (Susanna);
            Salomaa (Figaro); Nafé (Cherubino); Jones (Marcellina);
            Giminez (Basilio); Feller (Bartolo); Argenta (Barbarina);
            Drottningholm Court Theater Chorus and Orchestra;
            Östman (Conductor)

1990   Hampson (Count); Te Kanawa (Countess); Upshaw (Susanna);
            Furlanetto (Figaro); Von Otter (Cherubino); Troyanos (Marcellina);
            Laciura (Basilio); Plishka (Bartolo); Grant (Barbarina);
            Metropolitan Opera Chorus and Orchestra; Levine (Conductor)

1991   Schmidt (Count); Cuberli (Countess); Rodgers (Susanna);
            Tomlinson (Figaro); Bartoli (Cherubino); Pancella (Marcellina);
            Clark (Basilio); Von Kannen (Bartolo); Leidland (Barbarina);
            RIAS Chamber Chorus/Berlin Philharmonic Orchestra; Bareboim (Conductor)

1991   Furlanetto (Count); Varady (Countess); Donath (Susanna);
            Titus (Figaro); Schmiege (Cherubino); Kallisch (Marcellina);
            Zednik (Basilio); Nimsgern (Bartolo); Kertesi (Barbarina);
            Bavarian Radio Chorus and Symphony Orchestra; Davis (Conductor)

THE MARRIAGE OF FIGARO

Videography

DG

Gilfry (Count); Martinpelto (Countess); Hagley (Susanna); Terfel (Figaro);
Stephen (Cherubino); McCulloch (Marcellina); Egerton (Basilio);
Feller (Bartolo); Backes (Barbarina); Clarkson (Antonio);
Monteverdi Choir/English Baroque Orchestra;
Thamin (Director);
Mille (Video Director);
Gardiner (Conductor)

SONY VHS

Raimondi (Count); Studer (Countess); McLaughlin (Susanna); Gallo (Figaro);
Sima (Cherubino); Lilowa (Marcellina); Zednik (Basilio); Mazzola (Bartolo);
Tannenbergerova (Barbarina); Gátti (Antonio); Kasemann (Curzio);
Vienna State Opera Chorus and Orchestra;
Miller (Director)
Large (Video Director)
Abbado (Conductor)

DG

Fischer-Dieskau (Count); Te Kanawa (Countess); Freni (Susanna);
Prey (Figaro); Ewing (Cherubino); Begg (Marcellina);
Van Kesteren (Basilio); Montarsolo (Bartolo); Perry (Barbarina);
Vienna Philharmonic Orchestra;
Böhm (Conductor)
A film by Jean-Pierre Ponnelle

Phillips

Wahlgreen (Count); Lindenstrand (Countess); Resick (Susanna);
Samuelsson (Figaro); Biel (Cherubino); Mang-Habashi (Marcellina);
Lilliequist (Basilio); Saedén (Bartolo); Larsson (Barbarina);
Drottningholm Cojurt Theatre Chorus and Orchestra;
Järvefelt (Director);
Olofsson (Video Director);
Östman (Conductor)

DICTIONARY OF OPERA AND MUSICAL TERMS

Accelerando - Play the music faster, but gradually.

Adagio - At slow or gliding tempo, not as slow as Largo, but not as fast as Andante.

Agitato - Restless or agitated.

Allegro - At a brisk or lively tempo, faster than Andante but not as fast as Presto.

Andante - A moderately slow, easy-going tempo.

Appoggiatura - An extra or embellishing note preceding a main melodic note or tone. Usually written as a note of smaller size, it shares the time value of the main note.

Arabesque - Flourishes or fancy patterns usually applying to vocal virtuosity.

Aria - A solo song usually structured in a formal pattern. Arias generally convey reflective and introspective thoughts rather than descriptive action.

Arietta - A shortened form of aria.

Arioso - A musical passage or composition having a mixture of free recitative and metrical song.

Arpeggio - Producing the tones of a chord in succession but not simultaneously.

Atonal - Music that is not anchored in traditional musical tonality; it uses the chromatic scale impartially, does not use the diatonic scale and has no keynote or tonal center.

Ballad Opera - 18th century English opera consisting of spoken dialogue and music derived from popular ballad and folksong sources. The most famous is *The Beggar's Opera* which was a satire of the Italian opera seria.

Bar - A vertical line across the stave that divides the music into units.

Baritone - A male singing voice ranging between the bass and tenor.

Baroque - A style of artistic expression prevalent in the 17th century that is marked generally by the use of complex forms, bold ornamentation, and florid decoration. The Baroque period extends from approximately 1600 to 1750 and includes the works of the original creators of modern opera, the Camerata, as well as the later works by Bach and Handel.

Bass - The lowest male voices, usually divided into categories such as:

> **Basso buffo -** A bass voice that specializes in comic roles like Dr. Bartolo in Rossini's *The Barber of Seville*.

> **Basso cantante** - A bass voice that demonstrates melodic singing quality rather than comic or tragic: King Philip in Verdi's *Don Carlos*.

> **Basso profundo -** the deepest, most profound, or most dramatic of bass voices: Sarastro in Mozart's *The Magic Flute*.

.**Bel canto** - Literally "beautiful singing." It originated in Italian opera of the 17th and 18th centuries and stressed beautiful tones produced with ease, clarity, purity, evenness, together with an agile vocal technique and virtuosity. Bel canto flourished in the first half of the 19th century in the works of Rossini, Bellini, and Donizetti.

Cabaletta - Typically a lively bravura extension of an aria or duet that creates a climax. The term is derived from the Italian word "cavallo," or horse: it metaphorically describes a horse galloping to the finish line.

Cadenza - A flourish or brilliant part of an aria commonly inserted just before a finale.

Camerata - A gathering of Florentine writers and musicians between 1590 and 1600 who attempted to recreate what they believed was the ancient Greek theatrical synthesis of drama, music, and stage spectacle; their experimentation led to the creation of the early structural forms of modern opera.

Cantabile - An expression indication urging the singer to sing sweetly.

Cantata - A choral piece generally containing Scriptural narrative texts: Bach Cantatas.

Cantilena - A lyrical melodic line meant to be played or sung "cantabile," or with sweetness and expression.

Canzone - A short, lyrical operatic song usually containing no narrative association with the drama but rather simply reflecting the character's state of mind: Cherubino's "Voi che sapete" in Mozart's *The Marriage of Figaro.* Shorter versions are called canzonettas.

Castrato - A young male singer who was surgically castrated to retain his treble voice.

Cavatina - A short aria popular in the 18th century without the da capo repeat section.

Classical Period - The period between the Baroque and Romantic periods. The Classical period is generally considered to have begun with the birth of Mozart (1756) and ended with Beethoven's death (1830). Stylistically, the music of the period stressed clarity, precision, and rigid structural forms.

Coda - A trailer or tailpiece added on by the composer after the music's natural conclusion.

Coloratura - Literally colored: it refers to a soprano singing in the bel canto tradition with great agility, virtuosity, embellishments and ornamentation: Joan Sutherland singing in Donizetti's *Lucia di Lammermoor.*

Commedia dell'arte - A popular form of dramatic presentation originating in Renaissance Italy in which highly stylized characters were involved in comic plots involving mistaken identities and misunderstandings. The standard characters were Harlequin and Colombine: The "play within a play" in Leoncavallo's *I Pagliacci.*

Comprimario - A singer portraying secondary character roles such as confidantes, servants, and messengers.

Continuo - A bass part (as for a keyboard or stringed instrument) that was used especially in baroque ensemble music; it consists of a succession of bass notes with figures that indicate the required chords. Also called *figured bass, thoroughbass.*

Contralto - The lowest female voice derived from "contra" against, and "alto" voice, a voice between the tenor and mezzo-soprano.

Countertenor, or male alto vocal range - A high male voice generally singing within the female high soprano ranges.

Counterpoint - The combination of one or more independent melodies added into a single harmonic texture in which each retains its linear character: polyphony. The most sophisticated form of counterpoint is the fugue form in which up to 6 to 8 voices are combined, each providing a variation on the basic theme but each retaining its relation to the whole.

Crescendo - A gradual increase in the volume of a musical passage.

Da capo - Literally "from the top": repeat. Early 17th century da capo arias were in the form of A B A, the last A section repeating the first A section.

Deus ex machina - Literally "god out of a machine." A dramatic technique in which a person or thing appears or is introduced suddenly and unexpectedly; it provides a contrived solution to an apparently insoluble dramatic difficulty.

Diatonic - Relating to a major or minor musical scale that comprises intervals of five whole steps and two half steps.

Diminuendo - Gradually getting softer, the opposite of crescendo.

Dissonance - A mingling of discordant sounds that do not harmonize within the diatonic scale.

Diva - Literally a "goddess"; generally refers to a female opera star who either possesses, or pretends to possess, great rank.

Dominant - The fifth tone of the diatonic scale: in the key of C, the dominant is G.

Dramma giocoso - Literally meaning amusing, or lighthearted. Like tragicomedy it represents an opera whose story combines both serious and comic elements: Mozart's *Don Giovanni.*

Falsetto - Literally a lighter or "false" voice; an artificially produced high singing voice that extends above the range of the full voice.

Fioritura - Literally "flower"; a flowering ornamentation or embellishment of the vocal line within an aria.

Forte, Fortissimo - Forte (*f*) means loud: mezzo forte (*mf*) is fairly loud; fortissimo (*ff*) even louder, and additional *fff*'s indicate greater degrees of loudness.

Glissando - A rapid sliding up or down the scale.

Grand Opera - An opera in which there is no spoken dialogue and the entire text is set to music, frequently treating serious and dramatic subjects. Grand Opera flourished in France in the 19th century (Meyerbeer) and most notably by Verdi (Aida): the genre is epic in scale and combines spectacle, large choruses, scenery, and huge orchestras.

Heldentenor - A tenor with a powerful dramatic voice who possesses brilliant top notes and vocal stamina. Heldentenors are well suited to heroic (Wagnerian) roles: Lauritz Melchoir in Wagner's *Tristan und Isolde.*

Imbroglio - Literally "Intrigue"; an operatic scene with chaos and confusion and appropriate diverse melodies and rhythms.

Largo or larghetto - Largo indicates a very slow tempo; Larghetto is slightly faster than Largo.

Legato - Literally "tied"; therefore, successive tones that are connected smoothly. Opposing Legato would be Marcato (strongly accented and punctuated) and Staccato (short and aggressive).

Leitmotif - A short musical passage attached to a person, thing, feeling, or idea that provides associations when it recurs or is recalled.

Libretto - Literally "little book"; the text of an opera. On Broadway, the text of songs is called "lyrics" but the spoken text in the play is called the "book."

Lied - A German song; the plural is "lieder." Originally German art songs of the 19th century.

Light opera, or operetta - Operas that contain comic elements but light romantic plots: Johann Strauss's *Die Fledermaus.*

Maestro - From the Italian "master": a term of respect to conductors, composers, directors, and great musicians.

Melodrama - Words spoken over music. Melodrama appears in Beethoven's *Fidelio* but flourished during the late 19th century in the operas of Massenet (*Manon*). Melodrama should not be confused with melodrama when it describes a work that is characterized by extravagant theatricality and by the predominance of plot and physical action over characterization.

Mezza voce - Literally "medium voice," or singing with medium or half volume; it is generally intended as a vocal means to intensify emotion.

Mezzo-soprano - A woman's voice with a range between that of the soprano and contralto.

Molto - Very. Molto agitato means very agitated.

Obbligato - An elaborate accompaniment to a solo or principal melody that is usually played by a single instrument.

Octave - A musical interval embracing eight diatonic degrees: therefore, from C to C is an octave.

Opera - Literally "a work"; a dramatic or comic play combining music.

Opera buffa - Italian comic opera that flourished during the bel canto era. Buffo characters were usually basses singing patter songs: Dr. Bartolo in Rossini's *The Barber of Seville,* and Dr. Dulcamara in Donizetti's *The Elixir of Love.*

Opéra comique - A French opera characterized by spoken dialogue interspersed between the arias and ensemble numbers, as opposed to Grand Opera in which there is no spoken dialogue.

Operetta, or light opera - Operas that contain comic elements but tend to be more romantic: Strauss's *Die Fledermaus,* Offenbach's *La Périchole*, and Lehar's *The Merry Widow.* In operettas, there is usually much spoken dialogue, dancing, practical jokes, and mistaken identities.

Oratorio - A lengthy choral work, usually of a religious or philosophical nature and consisting chiefly of recitatives, arias, and choruses but in deference to its content, performed without action or scenery: Handel's *Messiah.*

Ornamentation - Extra embellishing notes—appoggiaturas, trills, roulades, or cadenzas—that enhance a melodic line.

Overture - The orchestral introduction to a musical dramatic work that frequently incorporates musical themes within the work.

Parlando - Literally "speaking"; the imitation of speech while singing, or singing that is almost speaking over the music. It is usually short and with minimal orchestral accompaniment.

Patter - Words rapidly and quickly delivered. Figaro's Largo in Rossini's *The Barber of Seville* is a patter song.

Pentatonic - A five-note scale, like the black notes within an octave on the piano.

Piano - Soft volume.

Pitch - The property of a musical tone that is determined by the frequency of the waves producing it.

Pizzicato - A passage played by plucking the strings instead of stroking the string with the bow.

Polyphony - Literally "many voices." A style of musical composition in which two or more independent melodies are juxtaposed in harmony; counterpoint.

Polytonal - The use of several tonal schemes simultaneously.

Portamento - A continuous gliding movement from one tone to another.

Prelude - An orchestral introduction to an act or the whole opera. An Overture can appear only at the beginning of an opera.

Presto, Prestissimo - Very fast and vigorous.

Prima Donna - The female star of an opera cast. Although the term was initially used to differentiate between the dramatic and vocal importance of a singer, today it generally describes the personality of a singer rather than her importance in the particular opera.

Prologue - A piece sung before the curtain goes up on the opera proper: Tonio's Prologue in Leoncavallo's *I Pagliacci*.

Quaver - An eighth note.

Range - The divisions of the voice: soprano, mezzo-soprano, contralto, tenor, baritone, and bass.

Recitative - A formal device that that advances the plot. It is usually a rhythmically free vocal style that imitates the natural inflections of speech; it represents the dialogue and narrative in operas and oratorios. Secco recitative is accompanied by harpsichord and sometimes with cello or continuo instruments and *accompagnato* indicates that the recitative is accompanied by the orchestra.

Ritornello - A short recurrent instrumental passage between elements of a vocal composition.

Romanza - A solo song that is usually sentimental; it is usually shorter and less complex than an aria and rarely deals with terror, rage, and anger.

Romantic Period - The period generally beginning with the raiding of the Bastille (1789) and the last revolutions and uprisings in Europe (1848). Romanticists generally found inspiration in nature and man. Beethoven's *Fidelio* (1805) is considered the first Romantic opera, followed by the works of Verdi and Wagner.

Roulade - A florid vocal embellishment sung to one syllable.

Rubato - Literally "robbed"; it is a fluctuation of tempo within a musical phrase, often against a rhythmically steady accompaniment.

Secco - The accompaniment for recitative played by the harpsichord and sometimes continuo instruments.

Semitone - A half-step, the smallest distance between two notes. In the key of C, the notes are E and F, and B and C.

Serial music - Music based on a series of tones in a chosen pattern without regard for traditional tonality.

Sforzando - Sudden loudness and force; it must stick out from the texture and provide a shock.

Singspiel - Early German musical drama employing spoken dialogue between songs: Mozart's *The Magic Flute*.

Soprano - The highest range of the female voice ranging from lyric (light and graceful quality) to dramatic (fuller and heavier in tone).

Sotto voce - Literally "below the voice"; sung softly between a whisper and a quiet conversational tone.

Soubrette - A soprano who sings supporting roles in comic opera: Adele in Strauss's *Die Fledermaus*, or Despina in Mozart's *Così fan tutte*.

Spinto - From the Italian "spingere" (to push); a soprano having lyric vocal qualities who "pushes" the voice to achieve heavier dramatic qualities.

Sprechstimme - Literally "speak voice." The singer half sings a note and half speaks; the declamation sounds like speaking but the duration of pitch makes it seem almost like singing.

Staccato - Short, clipped, rapid articulation; the opposite of the caressing effects of legato

Stretto - A concluding passage performed in a quicker tempo to create a musical climax.

Strophe - Music repeated for each verse of an aria.

Syncopation - Shifting the beat forward or back from its usual place in the bar; it is a temporary displacement of the regular metrical accent in music caused typically by stressing the weak beat.

Supernumerary - A "super"; a performer with a non-singing role: "Spear-carrier."

Tempo - Time, or speed. The ranges are Largo for very slow to Presto for very fast.

Tenor - Highest natural male voice.

Tessitura - The general range of a melody or voice part; but specifically, the part of the register in which most of the tones of a melody or voice part lie.

Tonality - The organization of all the tones and harmonies of a piece of music in relation to a tonic (the first tone of its scale).

Tone Poem - An orchestral piece with a program; a tscript.

Tonic - The keynote of the key in which a piece is written. C is the tonic of C major.

Trill - Two adjacent notes rapidly and repeatedly alternated.

Tutti - All together.

Twelve tone - The 12 chromatic tones of the octave placed in a chosen fixed order and constituting with some permitted permutations and derivations the melodic and harmonic material of a serial musical piece. Each note of the chromatic scale is used as part of the melody before any other note gets repeated.

Verismo - Literally "truth"; the artistic use of contemporary everyday material in preference to the heroic or legendary in opera. A movement from the late 19th century: *Carmen.*

Vibrato - A "vibration"; a slightly tremulous effect imparted to vocal or instrumental tone for added warmth and expressiveness by slight and rapid variations in pitch.